Taming Your Inner Tyrant:

A Path to Healing Through Dialogues with Oneself

by
Patty de Llosa

"There is no abyss, however deep,
no cliff, however high,
no labyrinth, however twisted,
that is not a way."
                    Talking with Angels

ISBN: 978-0-9822323-1-6

Library of Congress Control Number: 2011906351

A Spiritual Evolution Press
8 Luccarelli Drive
Holmdel, New Jersey 07733
www.aSpiritualEvolution.com

Dedicated to my many teachers and especially to G. I. Gurdjieff, who first called my attention to our Inner Tyrant and the many little 'i's, or personas, that move us, unaware.

To Jeanne de Salzmann, who lit my path toward the development of consciousness.

And to C. G. Jung and Marion Woodman, who helped me discover what I'd long undervalued in myself.

"Jesus Christ and all the other prophets sent from Above spoke of the death which might occur even during life...the death of that 'Tyrant' from whom proceeds our slavery in this life..."

G. I. Gurdjieff, *All and Everything*

"The tyrant is the man who narrows the scope of life, in other words creates a hell out of human life..."

Northrop Frye, *Late Notebooks, Vol. V*

Table of Contents

Introduction

"So long as we are blind to our inner tyrant, we blame an outer tyrant, some person or some system, for victimizing us. That maintains the split because victim and tyrant are dependent on each other, and together they must be healed."
Marion Woodman, *The Ravaged Bridegroom*

Do you too have an inner Tyrant, a hypercritical judge who monitors your every word and action, and tells you what's wrong with you? I do. He ruled my inner world for many years. Sometimes he was just mean and bossy, but most of his attacks were damaging, convincing me I was pretty stupid and my efforts worthless.

For a long time I thought he was the voice of my conscience, my better self, which meant if I didn't obey him I'd be "in the wrong." But when my marriage fell apart and I had to fend for myself and my three children, the physical and mental distress he inflicted on me became too much to bear. I sought help through a Jungian exercise called *Active Imagination*, a psychological experiment that attempts to bridge communication between our conscious selves and the unconscious world within. It offered me a path to a more positive relationship with my Tyrant and with other inner personas I discovered along the way. In other words, with myself.

My confrontation with my inner Tyrant began after I'd left my husband in Peru and returned to live in New York City. As a single mother—sandwiched between my job as managing editor of a fabric magazine and care for the three children who gave my life meaning—I was mired in an emotional swamp of guilt and self-accusation, as well as in physical pain. All day long an inner Judge harassed me, criticizing everything I did. At night he ruled my dreams as the cruel Tyrant of a police state.

In search of help, I began to read psychology books, starting with Jungian analyst Marion Woodman. When I read that "on some level the wounders and the wounded are one" (*The Ravaged Bridegroom*), I was horrified! "How could that be?" I asked. "One stabs, the other bleeds!" But even as my mind demanded to know how attacker and victim could ever be related to each other, the rest of me dissolved into tears. Deep in my heart I realized I could no longer run away from all I disapproved of in myself. Like Orestes in the Greek tragedy, I was pursued by the Furies.

Those unforgiving creatures gave me years of chronic pain. But it was only in mid-life that I thought to ask them: "Why are you after me?" Then, as I dialogued with my inner Tyrant, my life slowly began to change. I learned that I'd turned my back on certain aspects of myself because they seemed sinful or unacceptable. But in order to arrive at some semblance of inner peace I would have to build a relationship with them, find a common ground. And when I did, healing began.

Psychiatrist C. G. Jung says the first half of a person's life belongs to the development of the ego—education, finding a place in the world, job success, raising a family. But when we enter midlife as mature men and women, whether or not we've managed to live our dream, our enthusiasm for dancing to the drumbeat of success and power recedes. We turn to the depths of our own nature to seek the meaning of our lives.

As we question what it's all about, we may be astonished to discover that most of what moves us to do and to be is like an iceberg, nine-tenths hidden from our view. We contain many things, including what Jung calls the Transpersonal Self—not the small self we live with daily, but an inner guide from a larger psychic world.

Then how to deal with the wounds of life? Rather than dissolve into self-pity, bury ourselves in distractions, or dedicate ourselves blindly to getting stuff done, we can confront our personal Furies and even attempt an exchange with them. Perhaps someday they'll be transformed into the peaceful Eumenides. That's what happened at the end of Orestes' story, with the help of the gods. And it happened to me.

The dilemma that confronted me was how to digest all I'd lived through? The word *digest* was especially apt when I finally realized that my inability to process my life triggered more pain in my digestive system than the food I ate. My body suffered what the rest of me refused to accept. First slight discomfort—a queasy feeling—then nausea from time to time, followed by four years of intermittent daily reflux pain.

Acid-blockers like Tagamet, then Prilosec, provided some relief. Meditation temporarily quieted the pain. So did swimming. But it always came back the next day. Tai Chi, which I'd studied for many years, was indispensable when I became depressed. I'd waken in anguish at the emptiness inside, splash cold water on my face, and begin fifteen minutes of "meditation in motion." Only then could I move into the day with a modicum of intelligence for the many tasks ahead.

Two messages from books I helped translate into Spanish informed my attempts to understand what was going on. Sri Anirvan in *To Live Within* said: "Man is at the same time the cat that eats the mouse and the mouse devoured by the cat, for these are the two ways in which life comes toward us." And Jesus invited his followers to give up all pretence in *The Gospel of Thomas*: "Do not lie," he said. "And do not do what you hate." So I strove to accept that in any life situation I'm either mouse or cat, and tried hard neither to lie nor to do what I hated.

But wait a minute! Those were my dedicated conscious efforts to be a good human being in the face of life's stormy weather. However, as I turned toward an unconscious, unknown world inside me, I discovered that was only the tip of the iceberg. Beneath my conscious mind, the situation was very different. Too busy trying to do my best, I'd forgotten to ask: "What am I doing this for?" That left a huge gap between the person I wanted to be, even struggled very hard to be, and the person I was and am. Perhaps trying so hard evoked my inner Tyrant. But it also created the path along which I moved toward healing.

Unable to figure it all out in my head, I decided to make Jung's Active Imagination experiment and dialogue with my severest critic. The medium for this interchange can be painting, sculpting, writing, dancing, musical composition, or any means of self-expression in which the controlling consciousness plays second fiddle to the world below the mind. Dreams, images and feeling states, as well as bodily reactions, bring what's hidden in our unconscious into everyday awareness. So a dialogue between our conscious and unconscious psyche, through any creative medium, helps us learn more about the personality fragments or "complexes" which influence our actions, whether we're aware of them or not.

As Jungian therapist Robert Johnson defines them in *Living Your Unlived Life*, complexes are "clusters of experiential energy that hold us to repetitious patterns of response." They limit our freedom and tie us down to the past. Hidden from us, they motivate or punish without our suspecting their power. Only when we recognize and differentiate them from the person we consciously believe ourselves to be, do we begin to awaken to the scope of their influence.

To begin the Active Imagination process, you focus on an emotional reaction or a disturbing dream figure, offer it a listening mind or hand and allow it to express itself through you. That means letting the brush or words move on the paper, the clay form itself between your fingers, or the body go freely into movement.

The exercise calls for free expression without putting on your mental brakes. Inevitably, your conscious mind will try to dominate, correct or deny any manifestations that appear. While it's important for the mind to stay present as a witness, you try to focus on whatever's flowing from an unknown source. That way, a part of yourself you've never been aware of can manifest itself while you watch. "The essential thing is to differentiate oneself from these unconscious contents by personifying them," Jung points out, "and at the same time to bring them into relationship with consciousness. (That is) the technique for stripping them of their power." (*Memories, Dreams, Reflections*)

Although I doubted anything could allay the physical and emotional pain that attacked me every day, I sat at my computer, determined to try. My inner journalist, who prided herself on a probing mind that couldn't be taken in by claptrap, firmly announced: "This is ridiculous! It's me talking to me! How could anything new possibly come of it?" However, I'd read that Jung himself had the same doubts: "I was voluntarily submitting myself to emotions of which I could not really approve, and I was writing down fantasies which often struck me as nonsense, and toward which I had strong resistances." *(MDR)*

Well, if he could try it, so could I. And if it worked for him, maybe it would work for me! Determined to suspend incredulity, I closed my eyes, made an intentional effort to relax and typed out a question to the inner Tyrant: "Who are you?" Then I pressed the CAPS LOCK key and wrote down whatever comments surged up, as I tried not to let my conscious mind interfere.

The first responses were shocking. Accusatory words assaulted me, even as they revealed me to myself in unexpected ways. And, over time, a broader inner panorama opened up as a whole cast of characters emerged from the dark side of my being.

The Tyrant came first. Then a Frightened Child appeared, running away from him as fast as she could. Soon a Nazi Terrorist and a Wild Savage invaded my dreams as they tortured me or cut me up into body parts. During the day, a Slave-Driver whipped me along to keep me involved in useful activity while Superman, an imaginary companion of my childhood, urged me on to successful outcomes even though my outraged digestive system demanded a slower pace. Then came the Hero, Mrs. Rigid, the Ferret, the Editor, the Forgetful Child, the Woman in a Coma and the Lord of Discipline.

These personality fragments lived small separate lives in me. Each of them surfaced at different moments to play a part on the living stage of my days and nights. Jungian therapist Marie-Louise von Franz put it very well in *The Way of the Dream:* "Our field of consciousness is entered all day long by complexes…If we watch ourselves, we are many people…One of the aims of psychology is to help people to get on with their inner family of souls without being possessed by them."

As I spoke with each member of my "family of souls," I became gradually less possessed by their power to make me act compulsively. Books and workshops kept me company in this lonely endeavor. Analyst James Hillman was especially encouraging in *Healing Fiction*: "Entering one's interior story takes a courage similar to starting a novel. We have to engage with persons whose autonomy may radically alter, even dominate, our thoughts and feelings, neither ordering these persons about nor yielding to them full sway. Fictional and factual, they and we are drawn together like threads into a mythos, a plot, until death do us part. It is a rare courage that submits to this middle region of psychic reality where the supposed surety of fact and illusion of fiction exchange their clothes."

Soon firm attitudes I'd always thought were mine were revealed as fragmentary points of view. And, somewhere along the way, another voice began to emerge from the dialogues, along with a growing conviction that I wasn't alone in my pain, anger and frustration. Behind these rude and critical fragments, someone central in me was at work. A more permanent presence in this inner drama emerged to witness the performance of my cast of characters. Jung calls it the Self.

Although this sounds like a book on psychology, let me say right away that I'm not a therapist. It was written to share my discoveries with others and reveal how I managed to digest my indigestible life and heal the pain I'd refused to admit was tormenting me. As I did so, two lives finally connected with each other in me: that of a Seeker of consciousness and that of an unrecognized inner Other.

They lived in conflict for a long, painful time while I explored their needs and wants as best I could. Whether I identified them as personality and essence, *ego* and *id*, or wounder and wounded mattered little. No words could lessen the daily bouts of pain. No "thinking about it" could resolve my inner warfare. It was my dialogues with these fragmented selves that piloted me out of an emotional swamp and into a more balanced life.

At first, the only relief they brought me was a temporary easing of physical pain. I suffered through emptiness and depression as well as moments of new discoveries. I worked hard at proving myself, then at hating myself, and finally at forgiving myself. But when the scolding voices became more informational and their suggestions more practical, I learned that the unconscious reflects one's conscious attitude toward it. Once I began to respect these unexplored depths in myself, the dynamics shifted. Finally, to my infinite relief, I found myself on a two-way street. And with that realization came new hope.

If you too have suffered from painful inner division and the physical symptoms that accompany it, you may find these notes from my personal explorations useful. There are deep wells of untapped energy in the shadows below the mind for you to recover. And, for those who wish to undertake this experiment, I've suggested exercises at the end of each chapter that were useful to me in my rather blind search for freedom from pain and fear. May they help shorten your path to healing!

One: The Frightened Child

Disguised since childhood,
haphazardly assembled
from voices and fears and little pleasures,
We come of age as masks.

Rainer Maria Rilke, No one lives his life

I was in my early fifties when I discovered a little girl hidden in my depths. My life had fallen apart. I'd left my husband in Peru and returned with my children to New York where I scrounged around for an editorial job—anything to provide a roof overhead and healthy dinners for my kids. As managing editor of a trade magazine—little income, lots of pressure—there was barely time to rush from home to work to home in my frenetic attempt to be a Good Mother.

Depressed and in physical pain, I turned to Jung's Active Imagination exercise for help and began to dialogue with the tyrannical inner Judge who made my life miserable. But he soon constelled a second inner persona: that of a Frightened Child. I suspect there's a child within each of us, inevitably hurt in some way by life experiences. She may stumble into our conscious adult lives in surprising ways, bringing freshness and a taste of the joy of living. But she's probably terrified of the inner Tyrant, who prefers his world to remain as it has always been, under his negative thumb.

I thought I'd left that child far behind in my childhood, but here she was, amplifying the harsh times I was going through with sudden acts of sabotage. While I did my best to keep up the illusion that everything was ok, that I wasn't feeling desperate and hopeless inside, sometimes my careful mask would fall apart. Then I'd feel shame and a sense of inadequacy, as if a frightened child had been tripped up and exposed.

At last I realized I'd berated this clumsy, naïve, vulnerable side of myself all my adult years, hating my inability to be quick enough, smart enough, all-knowing enough to get the better of whatever challenge was facing me. Now something frightening was happening inside me, but I couldn't understand what the message was. And, anyway, how could I pay attention? "Maybe this is a frightened, desperate part of myself," I thought, "but I'm running under a full load. I just can't handle it."

In search of guidance, I began to attend lectures at the Jung Foundation, and soon found a therapist. When I told him about these upsetting visits from a frightened inner child, instead of calling me crazy, he suggested that she wasn't getting the attention she needed and perhaps even deserved. Nevertheless, I put it out of mind. No time to deal with a child's fear or comfort her in her grief. I had my own children to take care of!

A few months later, I confronted this unknown, yet well-known part of me at a health resort in Maine. My friend, who ran the resort, knew I was suffering from the breakup of my marriage and offered me the gift of a hypnotherapy session. Me? Hypnotism? You must be kidding! As a skeptical journalist, I scorned such nonsense! However, so as not to offend my friend, who believed in such things, I stretched out on the purple rug in the exercise room while a weird, longhaired young man told me to count quietly from one to ten.

He then told me I was becoming sleepy. "Ridiculous!" I thought, wide-awake with my eyes closed. He asked where I would like to go in my imagination. Pretending to go along with his nonsense, I chose the woods of my early childhood in the country. "You are walking down a path through the woods," he intoned in what he surely thought was a mesmerizing voice. "Who is coming to meet you?" To my surprise, my eight-year-old self appeared in my mind's eye, skinny and tough. She who loved to roam the woods and meadows, to fantasize in the garden and write poetry, had been left behind when we moved to the city, which I had passionately hated. Now she was leading me down the path, friendly but a bit contemptuous, since I clearly didn't know where I was going!

Guided by Longhair's intermittent questions, I followed her to a house in the woods and then into a room containing a large round table. "Who is sitting at it?" Longhair asked. Continuing my reverie, I was fascinated to see that there were six or seven people circled around it. Most striking was a grim-faced judge in black, an amorphous figure (man or woman?), emanating disapproval. Across the table, a red-caped, muscular Superman sat at ease, and next to him a pleasant, homey woman, among others.

At this point the hypnotherapist asked about my life situation, so I told him about the strain I was under. He ended our session by suggesting that maybe my inner Superman could help defend me from the scolding of the hypercritical Judge who was making my life miserable. At that moment, the same Judge was thinking how stupid this charade was, as "Mr. Hypnosis" slowly counted backwards from ten to one and pronounced me awake. But neither I nor my inner Judge could downplay the memory of the house in the woods where my personality fragments sat in eternal conference, or erase the image of the child who had led me to them.

Back home in the city, I catalogued this event as an interesting, if disturbing, vacation experience, and put it in a far corner of mind-storage. Nevertheless, unsettling situations continued to plague me. Were the different personas hidden in my inner world a lot more real than the ghostly figments I'd imagined them to be? Were they playing through me, in my present life, without my realizing it?

Psychiatrist Carl Jung suggests that if we could recognize the existence of these psychic fragments by becoming aware of how they manifest in us below the level of the conscious mind, and even try to have a conversation with them, we might arrive at new depths of understanding. "The essential thing," he wrote, "is to differentiate oneself from these unconscious contents by personifying them, and at the same time to bring them into relationship with consciousness." *(MDR)* This experiment came to be known as Active Imagination. By then, I felt I'd do anything to get out of the depressed emotional swamp I'd been sunk in for so long, so I decided to try it. My Tyrannical Judge wasn't hard to find. All day long, he shot arrows of criticism and negative judgments at me. So, one day, I sat at the computer and began to ask him questions, writing down his "answers" automatically as I tried not to react.

As these early dialogues took shape a couple of times a week, I became more aware of child-like inner reactions, appropriate for someone much younger. A new undercurrent of opposition to all I had to do interrupted my work, a resentful attitude about carrying out my duty. Someone in me seemed to say, "The hell with this! If I do all I have to do, there's no time for what I want to do!"

The situation came to a head at *Fortune*, on the first day of a new two-week cycle. I had to interview a lot of people for an up-coming article yet, all morning, an invisible but powerful force held me back from the plunge into my urgencies, resisting my efforts to get down to work. So instead of picking up the telephone to set up interviews, I turned to my overcrowded inbox, plucked out a magazine and began to read.

While I could feel momentary sympathy with whatever part of me refused to be drowned in "doing," this was scary. The deadline was very real. Yet obstacles appeared in my path all day long. Time was running out. Finally, I muttered out loud, "This can't go on!" As if in response, an inner voice replied: ***"YOU ARE THE MOTHER AS WELL AS THE CHILD."***

"OK," I answered. "I'm both mother and child. But this

child is messing up my work. It's got to stop! Don't mothers know best?" Again the voice: ***"DO MOTHERS LISTEN?"***

Shocked, I had to agree. I knew I wasn't a good listener, except on interviews. Who had time? Nevertheless, from then on I tried to be more attentive to my inner world, to notice these inner reactions, to become a receiving station for the child's voice. With this shift in attitude, she spoke to me more often and, to my growing discomfort, frequently acted out against my will. For example, sometimes she expressed herself as a kind of slithering out from under duty—full of the glee I associate with a child on a snow-day. Naturally I disapproved heartily, helpless that I couldn't discipline myself to have the "right" attitude. I'd tell myself, "I'm a grown-up with certain things I have to do and they should get done first. Only after that comes playtime." But she paid no attention.

At other moments, I felt weighed down by an indecipherable sadness. But when I queried what was wrong, no one answered. I'd hear a child weep inside but didn't know why she cried or what to do about it. What happened to her must have been buried in a past I couldn't recall. Yet it wasn't surprising that she felt hurt by events on which I'd turned my back, as I ploughed ahead to "get on with my life."

I turned to the Superman persona, as the hypnotherapist had suggested, hoping to defend myself from inarticulate suffering. This problem-solving side of me had dominated most of my adult life, helping me meet major challenges and attack every obstacle with zest. His point of view was that the only way to get ahead was to be a winner. But the nagging, childish resistance continued to confuse me, sweeping me into irrational actions without my recognizing where they were coming from until too late. That kid didn't give a hoot about my success, or doing what I "ought" to do.

One evening I came home from the office especially tired. Lots to do, but I couldn't force myself to "invest my time well." A physical resistance to cleaning up took over. Instead, the piles of clothes, dirty dishes, letters to be opened, bills to be paid made me mad. While the tug of war between duty and exhaustion was familiar, I'd never felt so angry before.

Suddenly my negativity was shattered by a thought. Could this too be the child? Why such resistance to bringing my world to order so I can get on with my life? It was more than I could stand. I cried out: "Child, what are you saying? Will you speak to me?"

And a voice shouted back: *"NO! NO! NO! I WILL NOT, NOT, NOT BE A PART OF THIS! I WILL NOT SOLVE PROBLEMS AND HAVE EVERYTHING HUNKY-DORY AND BE ABLE TO BE PROUD OF MYSELF FOR GETTING EVERYTHING IN ORDER, OR PLEASED WITH MYSELF FOR BEING A WINNER AGAIN."*

Shocked, I began my first dialogue with the child. As I wrote in my journal: *I'm sitting at my computer because I said I would and not because I know what I'm going to write. I recognize a child in me who has no place trying to do an adult job, who hurries down corridors or sits at my desk trying to tamp down her panic at the possibility of making mistakes. She bites her lip and slugs down tea to keep awake when the long hours of reading put her to sleep.*

Will you talk to me, little Patty?
WHY EVER NOT?

Well, I thought maybe you were hiding or didn't know what to say.
I DON'T.

Hide or know what to say?
BOTH.

Is there anything you want to say to me now, that you feel I don't usually hear?
ARE YOU KIDDING! WHEN AM I EVER HEARD?

Well, then here's your chance, what do you want or need? How do you see things from your point of view?
IT STINKS.

What stinks?
EVERYTHING.

Can you be clearer?
I'M PERFECTLY CLEAR.   IT'S YOU WHO ARE ALL MIXED UP!

That's true.   But I need some help and helping me could help you.
JEEPS-CREEPS, YOU GIVE YOURSELF A HARD TIME. WHY NOT CALL IT OFF, MAKE NICE, GIVE YOURSELF A BREAK.

How?
YOU'RE ALWAYS PUSHING, PUSHING, PUSHING.   WHY NOT STOP A WHILE AND LOOK INTO THE WATER. OR STARE AT A TREE INSTEAD OF GOING INTO ONE OF YOUR INNER FREEZES.

What can I do about your fear? What are you afraid of?
OF BEING EATEN.

Can you tell me more?   What do you have to do with my indigestion?
I AM YOUR INDIGESTION. YOU CAN'T DIGEST ME!

Well, is that a good thing or a bad thing?
'PENDS ON YOUR POINT OF VIEW.   IT GIVES YOU A HARD TIME FOR NOW.

How do you feel about it?
I WANT OUT OF YOUR PROBLEMS. I HAVE MY OWN PROBLEMS, BUT I'M ALWAYS HOLDING ON. YOU'RE ALWAYS HOLDING ON. IT STINKS. I'M SICK OF IT. HA! SO ARE YOU!

I don't know what to believe here. How are you my sickness?
WHO CARES WHAT YOU BELIEVE? I'M TELLING YOU THE TRUTH.

We need to get to know each other better. Can we be friends, companions?
WE ALREADY ARE. IT'S JUST THAT YOU NEVER LISTEN TO ME.

Help me to try...send me signals, will you?
HMMM.

Amazed that my effort to move out of conscious control and allow this inner voice to speak produced such a lively, spontaneous response in a long-forgotten idiom, I thought about our "conversation" for a long time. Clearly, I wasn't the person I thought myself to be. While I'd heard the voice of the Tyrant many times in my head, here was a surprising new point of view from a different quarter. I sensed instinctively that it deserved respect.

My "pushing" and "inner freezes" sounded familiar. It was my habit to press on, no matter how tired I was, in an effort to get things done. And when I pushed too far, I'd freeze up, passively sitting at my desk (or the kitchen table), unable to cope with so many demands at once. I'd just give up.

A few days later, in a headlong rush to cook supper, I spilled the millet I'd washed. It ran all over the kitchen floor in every direction—nice, round, wonderfully rolling, tiny pellets. But instead of shouting "Stupid!" at myself, as I usually did, I stood back and laughed. What an exciting mess!

Then I remembered how many times I'd tried to cook "special" dinners for my husband or my stepfather, often spilling, burning, hastily trying to improve on something that had already gone wrong. That must be the child again, trying ever so hard. But no matter how hard she tried, no matter how much she cared (and she cared very much!), nothing came out right. She was all thumbs.

We may not remember what happened in childhood that sent a fragment of ourselves off to an inner limbo, but we can give that part of us a voice. We can ask, "Why are you so angry?" or "Why do you act out and spoil things for me?" or "Why do you feel so alone, so unloved?" Then we can listen for an answer. Maybe there'll be an angry reaction or inarticulate weeping, as was often the case with me. But it needs to be heard. We need to accept the fact that a part of us we've been unaware of is in pain.

Is this child-self real? For a long time I thought of her as an unassimilated personality fragment left over from my childhood. However, years later, I discovered that Jung placed a very different value on the child persona. In one of his last books, he wrote: "In the individuation process, (the child archetype) anticipates the figure that comes from the synthesis of conscious and unconscious elements in the personality. It is therefore a symbol which unites the opposites; a mediator, bringer of healing, that is, one who makes whole." (*The Archetypes and the Collective Unconscious*)

My inner child had come through the woods to guide me down a new path, to help me become more whole.

If there is in each of us a divine child who can lead us toward wholeness, it's urgent that we wake up to him or her and begin a dialogue. What's more, I believe those of us who recognize the existence of this energy in ourselves have a duty toward it. Somehow we need to assure the frightened-child part that we're here to help, that we recognize her suffering, that she's no longer alone and misunderstood in an unfeeling world.

One way to begin to make contact with this inner child is to become alert to his or her manifestations in our daily life. When we stumble, say the wrong thing, feel helpless or angry at what we "have" to do, we can ask ourselves what's going on, in an open way. In my case, it was the early dialogues with the Tyrant that called my attention to the child. Then, when I accepted to listen to her point of view, she led me toward a new way of living and a new relationship with my inner cast of characters.

GET READY FOR SURPRISES
At the end of each chapter there are some explorations you can try. Keep a notebook at hand to write down details of your experiments and dialogues. Sometimes they make more sense or disclose new meanings when you read about them later, so even if they seem mysterious or offensive, note down what you tried and what happened.

RESPECT THE PSYCHIC FORCES YOU STIR UP IN THIS ADVENTURE
As you explore unknown territory, entering into contact with forces none of us understand, proceed with caution. You can only guess at how they move you from within without your awareness. The adventure may be fascinating and/or terrifying as you attempt to find a connection with that energy. But if your experiments lead you toward a sense of danger, find a therapist to work with who can provide objectivity grounded in reality.

HONESTY IS THE <u>ONLY</u> POLICY
Ask yourself, "Do I want to make contact? Is there someone inside me I've never listened to, never heard?" It's a scary thought and you are right to hesitate. This is not a game. These forces sometimes display a great sense of humor but the encounter with them is deadly serious and often painful. However, when there's a deep need to deal with pain and anger, as was my case, it's worth taking the risk.

GO BACKWARD TO GO FORWARD
If you decide to experiment, start by re-examining your childhood. Try to recall a few memorable situations you were in. Close your eyes and relive them if you can. Then call up a friend or family member who was present at that incident and ask them what they remember. Write down the primary details as if you were a reporter writing a newspaper article. Or, if words don't appear, try to paint a picture of the scene. Let pen or brush lead you without trying to interfere with its movement. Or put on music and dance the parts different people played in some watershed event from your past.

ACCEPT YOUR DOUBT
You don't have to believe this experiment will work. I certainly didn't! Let your doubt be there too. It's real. In fact, it's always a factor when we go into unknown territory. That's why we take a compass and fix landmarks in our minds so we can find our way back home. Home is in the present, where we anchor our inquiry as we go forth into the unknown.

FORGIVE YOURSELF AND OTHERS FOR YOUR PAIN
Children carry the presence we wish we hadn't lost. Because they are open, they bring their whole selves to every encounter, so it's inevitable that they get hurt. Many events that seem clear-cut to adults can torment children in unsuspected ways. Whatever we/they long ago chose to deny, or refuse to admit to consciousness today, we may have been deeply wounded by

someone or something. Both the pain and the denial must be respected. A child hasn't the life experience to understand why she's denied or even brutalized. So how can she forgive? But you can. You're now a grown-up.

STAY CONNECTED WITH BOTH WORLDS

You begin this experiment as an adult. Vow ahead of time not to lose consciousness of both worlds: that of the present moment and that of your childhood pain or anger. We all react in many ways that run the gamut of emotions from self-pity to rage. That's what it means to be human. But we don't want to be carried away by any one emotion. Like a scientist who undertakes an experiment without assuming the outcome, we move into unknown space.

TRUST THAT HELP EXISTS WITHIN YOU

Jung reminds us: "It is a striking paradox in all child myths that the 'child' is on the one hand delivered helpless into the power of terrible enemies and in continual danger of extinction, while on the other he possesses powers far exceeding those of ordinary humanity. This is closely related to the fact that though the child may be 'insignificant,' unknown, 'a mere child,' he is also divine." (*The Archetypes and the Collective Unconscious*). That divine child is still alive in you.

ADMIT TO ALL EMOTIONAL REACTIONS

Before I woke up to my inner child's existence, I met any sign of innocence, vulnerability or sense of inadequacy in myself, or others, with fear or anger. Any weakness threatened to damage the walls of the fortress I'd built up long ago to protect myself. Yet once I accepted the child's existence, the walls developed windows that provided light and helped me see into my former blindness. Once I realized she wasn't old enough to meet all the Superman demands I made on myself, I had to ask: "Why am I so angry at her mistakes? Why do I shout at her and want to punish her/me when we're doing our best?"

STOP SCOLDING YOURSELF

If you discover, as I did, that you tend to judge a frightened part of yourself or meet it with anger, ask, "What did I demand of this frightened child? Why did I expect him/her to know what to do? Would any child be able to handle it?" You don't want a negative relationship to go on forever: you annoyed at yourself; the child-part fearful and confused. Nowadays, when I wake up to the goings-on of my inner child-presence, I pull back from scolding her. "After all," I tell myself, "Who would treat a living child in the accusing, punishing way I treat my inner self whenever I drop things or slip up? She doesn't need an angry critic. She needs someone who cares."

BEGIN A DIALOGUE WHEN YOU'RE READY

Start communicating first in little ways. Listen to comments you make to yourself and answer back. Or, if you find this difficult, check out your body language. What makes you smile? Or frown? Feel good or bad? Or want to dance? Maybe you'll hear voices as I did. If so, write them down. Little by little (or all of a sudden), a dialogue will begin. Don't force it. Don't dwell on it. A deeply hurt child must be treated gently. Listen to the complaints. Try to elicit a further response even if you don't agree.

FIND YOUR BEST PATH

As I said in the introduction, this Active Imagination dialogue with the unconscious parts of ourselves can be developed through several methods. I used words, writing down the answers to my questions. But some people find an easier path through painting, sculpture or dance. Jung, who had no idea what was going on at the time, began to construct miniature buildings, stone by stone, until he had built a whole model village.

IGNORE THE SCORN OF THE TYRANT

The important thing is not to let the sneers of that Implacable Judge—the Tyrannical ruler of my conscious mind who perhaps rules yours, too—eat away at your resolve. He will do his best to make *you give up this delicate attempt to connect with parts of yourself he refuses to believe in. If you hear his catcalls, pay no attention to them. Remember, he's only another fragment, even though he thinks he's in charge!*

Two: Two Adams and an Eve

"To imagine our own parents is not unlike thinking about Adam and Eve, for our own parents are to a large extent figures bigger than life, for good or ill, who live in the imagination less as memories and more as myths."

Thomas Moore, *Soul Mates*

To my child-self, Mother was an angel of love. My birth father, who went off with another woman when I was six months old, was The Bad Guy. My stepfather, who appeared a few years later, was Strict but Fun. Yet when, in midlife, I examined the tangled web of memories and reactions, I recognized at least two people—and probably more—that I called mother, and four or more fathers.

While Mother was a cornucopia of tasty delights, endless energy and positive attitude, once in a while a wicked witch hid in her body and scolded or punished me. Where did that other woman come from? That's the Bad Mother, often the stepmother in children's stories. She turns cruel for no clear reason, exercises inhuman power over her small and helpless charges, and uses them for her own self-affirmation.

Whether or not we're aware of it, such images stick with us. As adults, some of us cling to the image of the Bad Mother and erase any Good Mother kindnesses from our memories. Others blot the Bad Mother out of their personal history, or create a Witch that took over her body, as I did. Psychologically speaking, that's not far from the truth, once we catch sight of how inner complexes or persona figures can make people act against their conscious intentions.

What's important, now that we're adults, is not to figure out who was at fault when things went wrong, but to recognize that Mom and Dad are human. They have "good" and "bad" qualities like ours. So if we want to heal our own inner division, we need to reject those labels when they appear and work to understand our real mother and father, rather than the stereotype.

When, in mid-life, I let go of my angel images and sought out long-forgotten impressions of my mother, I discovered a woman I hardly knew, with all her faults and virtues, joy and pain. She and I had always been close. We shared a dedication to the world's great religious literature and the Gurdjieff teaching. She considered me her best friend (surely an eye-brow raiser to therapists), and I admired her as a brilliant psychologist who helped many people find a more meaningful life.

When, after 18 years of marriage, I separated from my husband and returned with my children to my parents' house, I became seriously depressed. Mother then told me for the first time of her own depression after my father deserted her, and of her Jungian analysis with Dr. Christine Mann. Intrigued, I borrowed her psychology books, joined the Jung Foundation and began to study widely.

I learned that, if we wish to explore our unconscious inner relationship with our parents, the first thing we must give up is the assumption that they "belong" to us. My mother had her own harsh tale to tell, the kind found in dark novels. She was two when her mother died, taken in reluctantly by her grandmother, who told her she was her mother. She overheard conversations full of innuendo between her grandparents and her five grown-up "sisters and brothers" — her aunts and uncles.

Deceit and half-truths were hidden in every family encounter. The small child began to suspect there was something really wrong with her, something unacceptable. But, as she grew up, she found solace in school, cheap seats in the peanut gallery of the famed Philadelphia orchestra. Saturday mornings at the public library were her happiest times, where she read fairytales to smaller children.

At age 12, Mother was sent to earn her keep wrapping packages in a department store basement until she became seriously anemic. When the family doctor prescribed rest and country air, she was sent to Atlantic City to breathe in that good sea atmosphere while taking care of her "sister's" three children. On her return, much to her joy, the doctor insisted she wasn't yet able to work a full day, so she was sent back to school. Even in her 90's, she declared: "that was the happiest day of my life."

When I.Q. tests exposed Mother's exceptional intelligence, the psychologist in charge of testing tried to adopt her. But by then she'd had enough of pseudo-parents and refused outright to belong to anyone. However, miraculously, a full scholarship to Alfred University was offered her. She was to live with the psychologist's husband, a professor there.

Halfway through her senior year, Mother's world crashed around her again. The psychologist accused her of trying to seduce the professor and arranged for the loss of her scholarship. Angry and betrayed, with a college degree only months away and $17 in her pocket, she took a bus to the nearest big town to look for a job. The "nice older man" at the front desk of the Rochester *Democrat* turned out to be the managing editor. He liked her gall and gave her a shot at cub reporting. She went on to prove herself in what was then a man's world, hired a few years later by the New York *American*. There, in her early twenties, she became both fashion editor (with trips to Paris) and Mother Manhattan (advice to the lovelorn).

However, raising a family meant much more to Mother than pursuing a career. She soon married an Associated Press reporter, and was abandoned by him a few years later during the Great Depression, with a toddler and an infant to raise alone. Once again she landed on her feet, as director of the writers' project for the Connecticut Work Project Administration (WPA). Later on, she turned to writing advertising copy at Benton & Bowles, where she met my stepfather.

How did she survive the hard times of her childhood and youth? Abetted by avid reading, she molded herself after the virtuous heroines of early 20th century children's literature. Always a fighter, never a complainer, she met every damaging attack on her right to be alive with the attitude of a warrior, which is surely what saved her from being destroyed. Nevertheless, although she became a deeply perceptive psychologist, she later admitted to me that she could never really trust anyone. She knew too much about human betrayal.

When I returned to New York, we began to write her story together. I sat at the computer while she reminisced, calling up images from a fading memory. Then, in her 90's, it was my turn to mother her and care for her as if for a child. Although it was harrowing for me to accept her helplessness, she was so filled with love that there were no boundaries between us.

That's how I found a new relationship with this Great Lady of my life. Loving mother, talented cook, wise woman who helped scores of people find their path—it was probably inevitable that I would want to mold myself after her because, in my view, she seemed to have it all. But, after she died, her diaries revealed a woman often uncertain of what to do and always critical of herself, whatever she decided.

I had two fathers, very different from each other, both of them larger-than-life. So, like many a little girl who has confused her daddy with God the Father, who thundered his disapproval of human frailty ever since He threw Adam and Eve out of Eden, I was easily squashed. I shrank from loud noises all my life. What tiny psyche could avoid being crushed by the power emanating from the first loud-voiced male in the house?

Jung tells us that: "The father…is the source of 'spirit' for the daughter. Unfortunately this source is often sullied just where we would expect clear water. For the spirit that benefits a woman is not mere intellect...it is an attitude, the spirit by which a man lives...Hence every father is given the opportunity to corrupt, in one way or another, his daughter's nature." C. G. Jung (Collected Works Vol 14).

My first indication that something was off kilter between me and my two fathers was the discovery that I couldn't call either of them "Father" or "Daddy." The words just wouldn't come. While both were highly intelligent, educated and demanding, comparisons stopped there. The biological Bad Guy reappeared infrequently, only long enough to awaken in me the feeling that I was somehow second-rate, "just a girl." He was profligate (four wives), irresponsible (four children whom he deserted when they were very young) and pretentious. He seldom paid our school bills, causing my mother endless financial anxiety. Yet, from time to time, he telephoned us to complain in an acutely sentimental voice: "I'm so lonely without you."

Our first adult reunion took place when I was a reporter for *Time.* He was clearly proud of that—it gave me meaning in his eyes. My own feelings were tangled in the strain of lunching with this now-stranger on my own turf at Rockefeller Center. Was he a threat? Did he care for me? His excuse for meeting was to give me Grandmother's sapphire ring, which she'd left me in her will. However, though it was often promised, I never saw it.

In the last few years of his life (he died at 96), I began a new relationship with him on yearly weeklong visits to his Florida house on the Gulf. A few steps from the main house, a little one-room studio provided just the R & R I needed from my pressured life as a journalist and mother in New York: private beach, all meals included. My only duty was to be agreeable at mealtimes, share stories of my interesting life at *Fortune,* and go to a few cocktail parties where he could show me off to his friends.

We exchanged resentments we'd held back for a lifetime. I felt he never cared about me because he seemed much more interested in my brother. He had been deeply hurt by my marriage announcement in the New York *Times*, which listed my stepfather instead of him. While some hidden part of me thirsted for father-affection, I was Very Careful not to be caught in an emotional trap. He was a mean man and I'd been wounded early. Yet to my surprise, although in childhood I'd been "just a girl" and he'd clearly preferred his three strapping sons, I'd now become his Only Daughter.

In his final year, suffering from cancer and sometimes unconscious from pain-reducing patches, he was often incoherent as he muttered in dreams and complained when awake. I'd sit by his bed and try gently to comfort him. The day I left, a clear message emerged out of his indecipherable moans: "Will you shut up!" These were his Last Words on earth. He died the following night.

My stepfather entered our family as "uncle" when I was two or three and soon became the real parent—dependable, ready to teach us, comfort us and help solve our problems. He loved me, teased me, cleaned my cuts and bruises, and sat by my bed all night when I had an inflamed appendix. Without doubt the opposite of the Bad Guy, he frequently condemned him for "what he did to your Mother." Hoping to please him, I changed my name to his when I got my first passport and listed him as my father in my marriage announcement. When I visited my birth father late in his life, I felt guilty and secretive, thinking the man who had replaced him in every way might feel betrayed.

An up-and-coming ad man at Benton & Bowles, my stepfather abandoned that career as he approached the height of success, to search for deeper meaning in his life. He put himself through medical school on money borrowed from friends, explaining in his book, *What Happened In Between: A Doctor's Story*: "a small worm continued to gnaw at my self-esteem. It seemed increasingly shameful to know so little and pretend so much."

As a doctor he was a practical, far-seeing student of the human condition, a gifted diagnostician and, later, president of the New York Heart Association. He was also a humble practitioner who refused to raise his prices when other doctors did, because medicine was about helping your fellow man. In private life, he was a talented mimic and soft shoe dancer, full of gusto and enthusiasm about food, people, history, thought, architecture.

It was when he was in his 80's that our relationship became difficult. Depressed by his wife's memory loss and his own growing blindness and aching limbs, he became an angry man. Although I tried to help as best I could, he was demanding and critical, and I, although full of sympathy for his situation, felt like a failure, unable to satisfy his needs.

My two Adams and an Eve represent both myth and reality in my life story. In the end, my mother, the Ideal Woman, became a beloved child. After many years of resentment of my birth father, I accepted how he was and cared for him in his last years. Ever grateful to my stepfather for taking on a young mother with two children and raising me as his own, I recognized that no matter how hard I tried to please him, I'd never measure up to his lofty standards. But I acknowledged that he held himself to them as well.

TAKE A WALK DOWN MEMORY LANE
As you did with your child-self in the first chapter, try to call up memories of various times with your parents, the happy ones, the sad ones, the angry ones. Which scenes are immediately called to mind? Can you relive them? What images still have the power to make you angry? Or sad? Or happy?

BECOME SLEEPING BEAUTY

Imagine your Mother as the Fairy Godmother in the Sleeping Beauty. What is there about that image that doesn't fit? How about the Queen mother who seems to have been pretty passive in the story? And is your father a King or a Handsome Prince come to rescue you from a century of sleep?

NOW BE HANSEL OR GRETEL

Cast Mom in the role of the Bad Stepmother or the Wicked Witch in Hansel and Gretel. Where and when does that fit? And was your father in any way similar to the hen-pecked husband who let his wife send his children off into the woods with the unconscious hope that they'd never come back?

OR DO BOTH APPLY?

Weigh the good and the bad memories and find a middle road if you can. It will probably be far nearer the truth than either extreme. Write your thoughts down from all these points of view and see if you come up with a new image, more complex, more real.

A TRIP HOME COULD BE USEFUL TO YOUR INNER SCIENTIST

A visit to your parents, if they are still alive, or other important members of your first family, would provide you with good material for study. You can then notice firsthand the tendency to fall into old habits, old attitudes, old arguments. You may also discover that, as you long suspected, they barely know you at all. They react to their memory of you, not the person you've become.

IT'S YOUR TURN TO BE THE ADULT IN THE RELATIONSHIP

Often when we visit our parents or other family members, we react to them in the same old ways. They do the same with us. It's not easy to go against the force of habit and the powerful influence of that dependent time when they were God and Goddess of our fate. But next time you visit them, perhaps you can experiment with a new conscious attitude. Sooner or later you need to become mother and father, or older brother and sister, to yourself.

LET GO OF BLAME

Whether or not the woman who raised you played the part of the Good or Bad Fairy and the first man in your life left you lost in the woods, stay with your own exploration. First take stock of your anger, hurt, shame or whatever it is, and admit to it fully. Even tell them about it if that seems useful. But don't waste too much time blaming them or yourself.

EXPECT FAMILY DYNAMICS TO COME INTO PLAY

Psychologists say as soon as we attempt change, old family patterns will try to reinsert themselves. That means when one family member tries to break away from his or her perceived "role," all the others will (unconsciously) do their best to get him or her back in line. You're programmed to play the part you always played within your family, but the light of consciousness can illumine the situation. Claim your right to be the new, now person you are, even if they aren't able to see you. While it may be unwise to inform them of their blindness, keep conscious track of everyone's reactions. Write it all down. You'll be helped when you read it later.

DON'T TAKE ANYTHING FOR GRANTED

The tendency to judge others as good or bad seeps into every exchange, so be alert to what's useful to your own search. The Good Fairy has drawbacks too. I suspect she needs a lot of praise and celebrating. Also, the frog has been known to turn into a Handsome Prince and the Wicked Witch into a fairy Godmother. Remember the Hag at King Arthur's Court? She became a beautiful young woman when the knight found the right answer to her question: "What does a woman want above all else?"

INVESTIGATE YOUR FAMILY'S HISTORY

Find out more about them. Ask parents, grandparents, aunts, uncles, cousins about their childhood and their parents. Perhaps they inherited charm or closed minds, psychic flaws, kindness or cruelty from their own parents. Maybe some of their traits (and yours) went several generations back. No matter how difficult your youth may have been, it will be a lot more rewarding to investigate your family's history than to resent them, even if you feel justified.

Three: Say Hello to the Pleaser

"Nearly every traumatized child ends up believing that s/he is in pain because s/he is fundamentally at fault… 'If only I can become 'good enough' then my pain will stop, and if I can't become 'good enough' then maybe I can hide my self well enough to stop the pain.'"
Donald Kalsched, (Interview in *Caduceus Journal*, 2006)

Each of us must deal in some way with the blows we receive in childhood. Whether they come from trauma, abuse or simple misunderstanding, we develop a habitual response to what we perceive as threats or criticism—an attitude that can last a lifetime. Some people go into an attack mode; others play the victim's part; still others enclose themselves in a safer inner world of their own. And there are those, like me, who sacrifice their inner equilibrium in an attempt to please others and ward off disapproval.

Why do children sacrifice their true core to please someone else? Many reasons. They feel powerless and unsure of themselves; they trust someone older; they're afraid of being wrong or being punished. But why should that matter now that we're adults? Put simply, the compulsion to please has become an unconscious habit.

When I realized in mid-life how hard I'd always tried to please, I was horrified at first. "How shameful!" I thought. "I've failed to respect my true self." But as I looked back and reviewed the pressures I'd felt as a child, I began to sympathize with the little girl I once was. She tried so desperately to meet the incomprehensible demands of a world she just couldn't figure out.

As with most children, my primary aim had been to please Mother, who had very high standards. It was also indispensable to please my older, stronger brother, who had his own agenda and sometimes found me useful. I seldom thought about The Bad Guy, my birth father. He was a shadowy image, seldom seen or heard from since he'd disappeared when I was a baby, but I knew he'd deserted us and preferred boys to girls, so I fell short from the start.

My "uncle," who later became my stepfather, demanded a high level of performance from himself and others. It seemed natural to work hard to please him. He could be a lot of fun when he entertained us with soft-shoe dances and songs from the Twenties, as well as doctoring our cuts and bruises. And he, too, carried a traumatic childhood, wounded by a father whose anger was legendary in the small town where he grew up.

With other grownups and school friends, I simply ached to be liked, to be included in the mysterious world that seemed so foreign. Since other people's needs or demands were often obscure, I desperately struggled to figure out how I could earn their approval or gratitude. And even when I thought I'd won them over, I never felt safe from criticism or judgment.

In my teens, this fear of disapproval or rejection played havoc with any hope of self-confidence. Remember the girl in the corner who changed the music or passed the trays of snacks around at parties? That was me. Shy and self-denigrating, I was attracted to boys who were commanding and sure of themselves even when, after the first flush of interest, I saw through the bravado to their self-preoccupation and self-doubt. This attraction to authoritative people persisted when I grew up, as an unconscious need for some "expert" to guide my decisions.

All the way into my middle fifties, my Pleaser persona went unrecognized. It was uncovered quite accidentally when I picked up a book called "*When I Say No, I Feel Guilty*" by Manuel J. Smith. Yeow! There I was, naked as I'd never been before! That was when I began to study my compulsion and ask how I offered myself to wounding.

Not long after, a friend came to visit. Her three-hour

barrage of talk exhausted me, so I asked my Inner Tyrant about this Pleaser habit:

Why do I allow myself to be depleted? Why do I make myself into an edible fungus for others to eat up at their pleasure?
LOOK HOW YOU LISTENED...CONCENTRATING EAGERLY ON EVERY WORD AS IF YOU WERE GOING TO GET AN EXAM ON IT THE NEXT DAY. WHY DO YOU LIVE SO FAR FROM YOURSELF?

Listen, you bum. I'm trying my best and it's pretty obvious that my best isn't good enough. But just how much do I have to dump on myself before I accept I'm the way I am and I just can't help it?
SURE. BUT LOOK HOW RESENTFUL YOU ARE NOW ABOUT BEING USED UP BY A CONVERSATION THAT'S CATHARTIC FOR THIS OTHER LADY BUT DOES NOTHING FOR YOU. IT'S GREAT FOR HER! BUT WHAT KIND OF BUSINESS ARE YOU IN?

What kind of business was I in? That startling question penetrated my self-protective blinders. It reminded me of the card game I'd played with my children in Lima, called *Nobody Knows Who They're Working For*, which had always seemed endless, as we won and lost cards in a meaningless exchange. What business was I in? Who was I working for? The questions resounded in me day after day, kept alive by new discoveries.

Whenever we uncover habits we don't like in ourselves, we try to change them as fast as possible. I longed to make a 180-degree turn in my personality then and there. But it didn't work. The roots of compulsions go deep. The only way to alter them is to connect with the origins of their energy in the unconscious world below the mind. That's why my conversations with my personas were so effective. Over time, they brought me to a new relationship with these unconscious attitudes as I became less vulnerable and more aware of them.

But the bestseller I'd read on guilt made it clear that these compulsions weren't uniquely mine, that many people are pleasers, not just me. As I delved deeper into psychology, I learned that such habits can even be traced back to previous generations. According to psychologists, children inevitably inherit the unlived life and unsolved problems of their parents and grandparents. That's why it's so important to study our family history, to learn how our antecedents dealt with their lives and relationships. It offers us an opportunity to help ourselves and our children become free of unnecessary behaviors and compulsions. As Jung pointed out, the best thing parents can do is to live their own lives to the fullest, and free their children from parental "baggage."

All of this set me to thinking: Did my Pleaser have deeper roots than my own life experiences? I knew that, in spite of my compulsion to please, I'd never suffered my mother's level of trauma. But if psychic damage passes from one generation to another, maybe I unconsciously absorbed her experiences of childhood abuse. Although she never talked about them, the effects had to be there among us as I grew up. What's more, family meant everything to her, as it later did to me. Perhaps that was why leaving my husband and breaking up my own family became such a sure recipe for guilty feelings.

Another aspect of the compulsion to please, as anyone who shares my addiction will know, is the agony of decision-making. Even minor choices were hard to make because I didn't dare put forward my own wants and needs. Tongue-tied when asked what I wanted to do, "What would you like to do?" was my only possible answer. "What movie shall we see tonight?" my husband might ask. "Which would you like to go to?" were the only words I could utter.

Looking for a way out of the inability to tell others what I wanted, I practiced voicing my preferences to myself. But it was hard work. All I could do was decide inwardly what I liked best before decisions were made. Then I could go along with what my friends wanted, but at least I knew what my own choices were.

When I shopped for clothes, I always took a friend along to tell me what I looked good in. As for deciding what to wear to the office, I habitually laid out my clothes at night for the following day, to avoid anguish and wasted time in the early morning. However one danger of checking out what others like without having an opinion of your own, is that you tend to become rigid. It gets harder and harder to choose what's appropriate for the moment. I discovered that when I bumped into another persona: Mrs. Rigid (see Chapter 11).

As I became more aware of my compulsive inner obligation to please others at the price of my own preferences, I asked: "What are *my* needs?" But I didn't listen long for answers. How could I include *me* in my busy life? With elderly parents, children and a fulltime job, it wasn't easy. Nevertheless, I began to swim twice a week and, as always, did Tai Chi exercises every day. I also began to look for indirect ways to fit in care for myself. For example, when I learned a dear friend had been taken to the hospital, I stifled my first reaction to rush there with fruit, chocolates and sympathy. Instead, I forced myself to stop at a park en route for ten minutes of Tai Chi. That way I felt grounded as I walked into the alienating hospital atmosphere to visit her.

Such grounding is essential. In fact, just as fear lessens in direct proportion to increased body awareness, so does the need to please recede when a strong sense of psychophysical presence appears in us. When we are present in body, mind and feelings, we become aware of the vibrating life within us, the breathing being. That permits us to see our compulsive habits more clearly.

Inevitably, as we discover aspects of ourselves we don't like, we tend to turn away in instant denial or rush toward instant (illusory) change. But if we can, instead, stay present to these habitual defensive reactions, a door to an inner world below our surface perceptions may open. What's more, each time we see a little more deeply into our "mechanics," we have a chance to change direction.

Imagine you're on a sailboat and fall asleep, or maybe you just don't know how to sail well. Suddenly you realize you're going in a wrong direction or you've "done the wrong thing." Hey! No time for recriminations or self-accusation! You're in a serious bind. Right now, in the midst of the confusion, you've got to put your hand on the tiller to change tack (shift the sails) as quickly as you can to avoid foundering! If you don't know how, you can look for an expert. (Lucky you, if there's one on board). Otherwise, you're on your own. Ahh! You managed it. What a relief! Now you're on a straight course toward where you wanted to go.

Of course the biggest problem with this analogy is that we often aren't sure where we want to go. If we are pleasers or self-doubters, instead of taking the time to figure it out, we ask around to discover what others think is the best place for us to be. Or, alternatively, we freeze in our tracks and stay very still until the boat capsizes or somebody else grabs the tiller of our lives.

I'm happy to inform those who share my Pleaser compulsions that change is possible. But you have to start by admitting to the tendency. That may be harder than you think. In any case, if pleasing others has been a dominant note in your life, and you are prepared to give it serious study, a brighter future beckons. Freedom and new energy may reward you if you can get to work.

Above all, don't get discouraged, even if, as you try to change, pleasing continues to be a habitual first reaction. To deal with it, ask yourself Baba Yaga's question in the Russian fairytale: "Are you doing this of your own free will or by compulsion?" (For more on this theme, see *The Maiden King*, by Marion Woodman and Robert Bly). Or, if that doesn't work for you, when the urge to make nice reappears, you can remind yourself who the Pleaser really is: an intruder in your psyche.

Although I was a prisoner of this compulsion for many years, a confrontation with that long-ignored little girl called me to account. One day, after I'd spent a lot of time and energy helping a friend, I felt exhausted. As I began to justify to myself why I had to do it, she lashed out at me:

I DON'T, DON'T, DON'T WANT TO BE A GOOD GIRL ANY MORE! DO YOU HEAR? DO YOU HEAR? DO YOU HEAR?

Yeow! What's that all about?
I FEEL CAUGHT IN MY OWN BLINDNESS, SWALLOWED IN SOMETHING I CAN'T SEE. I'M CAUGHT, CAUGHT, CAUGHT! WHY ARE YOU SO ENGAGED IN SUCCEEDING OR DOING IT RIGHT AS IF WHATEVER HAS TO BE DONE IS A MATTER OF LIFE AND DEATH? WHAT IS THIS COMMITMENT THAT PUTS EVERYBODY AND EVERYTHING FIRST AND ME LAST?

Appalled by what seemed an enormous offense against her innocence, I humbly asked:
Then what do you want me to say to people instead of trying to please them?
TELL THEM: "I LOVE! ISN'T THAT ENOUGH? DO I HAVE TO PLEASE YOU TOO?"

"I love. Isn't that enough?" The anguished cry of someone in me who loved and wanted to be loved in return for who she is, not what she does for you. That soul-deep plea pierced my heart and changed my life. And as soon as I probed for this Pleaser persona in my daily relationships, it became more visible. By giving it a name and form, I was able to differentiate it from the person I really am. You can do it, too.

WHAT KIND OF BUSINESS ARE YOU IN?

If you want to find out more about yourself, to heal your psychic wounds, then your aim is clear. But if you aren't sure these efforts are right for you, then you need to clarify for yourself what you really want. Ask yourself, do you do whatever you do in order to please others or because it seems right? Or, to use Baba Yaga's life-or-death riddle: Do you do it of your own free will or by compulsion?

WHO ARE YOU WORKING FOR?

As you begin to delve into the world below your conscious mind you could ask this question of your Inner Tyrant. His answers might surprise you. Then look at your relationship with other people. Is it fruitful and rewarding? Are you a pleaser like me? Or does some part of you avoid intimacy, hesitate to make friends?

"HOW'M I DOING?" VERSUS "HERE I AM"

Try to catch sight of which of these two modes of being-in-the-world you may be in at any particular moment. This exercise was particularly helpful to me as I caught myself wondering, again and again, what impression I was making on other people. So ask yourself often: Are you focused on how you look to others and what they think of you, or how you yourself really think and feel?

BECOME AN EXPERT ON YOURSELF

With the attitude of a scientist exploring new theories, write down in your notebook what you think you already know about yourself. Among other things, when do you try to please? Whom do you want to please? Why? Remind yourself that these are personality habits and don't reflect who you really are. They only indicate how you deal with what you've been dealt by life.

DON'T ATTACK YOURSELF

Beware of your own judgmental pronouncements and self-accusations. Refuse to accept them as God's truth. Defuse them. Such judgments are often attempts to escape the fire you've lit to illuminate your path toward the truth about yourself. Let yourself burn. It's called remorse and it brings transformative energy. As you digest your discoveries, you'll develop a more productive response. Hold your conscious mind open to learning more. As the Sufi poet, Rumi, said: "Out beyond ideas of wrongdoing and rightdoing, there is a field. I will meet you there." That's the field where you want to make these experiments.

BEGIN TO LISTEN TO YOUR INNER VOICES

There's a lot you already know about yourself that you don't tune into. When you've written down your own opinions and remembered other people's reactions to you, you can begin to ask your cast of characters what they know about you. They may have points of view that will startle you. Don't justify. Listen to the comments your mind makes, the ones we're often unaware of. If none appear, invite them. If an accusation comes at you, ask to have it explained. Tell the inner critics you want to understand why you do what they accuse you of. Ask them for help!

PREPARE TO BE HONEST

It's hard to listen to an unpleasant truth someone else tells you about yourself. What have others said about you? Did a friend (or enemy) make a comment that really hurt? Sometimes that's a clue. Was there some truth in it? It's much harder to accept what your own personality fragments say about you even when, somewhere deep down, you may already suspect it's true.

EXPERIMENT WITH GOING AGAINST YOUR HABIT

The hardest word for a pleaser to say is "no," which means you need practice. Lots of useful information will be stirred up if you can stomach the effort. So when you find yourself signing up one more time for more than you really want to do, or praising something you really think is second-rate, dare to tell the truth. Try it on small things at first. Listen to your own voice as you say, "I don't really want to do that;" "I don't think I like that color on you;" or "I bet you could do a better job if you tried harder."

STALL FOR TIME
If you're as yet unable to say "no," at least create a pause. Say: "I need to think it over and let you know tomorrow." People will respect you for that. It shows you take their request seriously. Give it a night's sleep and ask yourself next day whether you feel put out by the request. Unless it feels in some way fulfilling, try to say "no." Practice your "no" on little things to get the hang of it.

GIVE YOUR PERSONAS A NAME
Judge, Accuser, Tyrant, Terrorist, Pleaser, Little Friend of All the World, find a label for each of the fragments you dialogue with. That helps you to differentiate them from your own core of truth. They are members of the cast of characters in your human drama, some helpful, some hateful, some useful. Get to know them.

Four: Life as an Underdog

"Children…are trying to live two lives at once, the one they were born with and the one of the pace and among the people they were born into. The entire image of a destiny is packed into a tiny acorn, the seed of a huge oak on small shoulders."

James Hillman, *The Soul's Code*

Were you, too, one of the underdogs in a classroom, picked on by everyone? It's hard to understand why children can be so cruel to each other. Sometimes they imitate a parent or elder sibling. But it often seems to come from a competitive instinct, a group attack to keep the other guy down so we can stay on top. Even the bully is usually aggressive because someone bigger and stronger once gave him a hard time. Or maybe he suffered a traumatic experience that turned him into an attack dog.

At the age of eight, I was uprooted from the countryside where I had flourished, and forced to adjust to the alien noise and confusion of a big city. Probably I was sweet, simple and trusting, In any case, I soon became the butt of my 4th grade teacher, Miss P. When the children found they were free to explore cruelty, most of the class made fun of me. The worst part was the walk home when the boys would surround me across the street from the school, calling me names and trying to pull up my skirt.

Other humiliations followed. I loved writing poems but, when we were asked to read them out loud, everyone laughed at my treasures.   One girl befriended me—oh, brief hope of companionship!—only to desert me a few months later with the cruel words: "I only make friends with people nobody likes because I feel sorry for them."

However, worse was to come. Miss P. also taught the 5th and 6th grade, so the terror and isolation went on for two years and looked to last forever. The climax came in the last week of 5th grade when she decided I had been rude. I can't recall what I'd done to deserve punishment, but I'll never forget how she picked up her ruler, grabbed my hand and swatted my palm soundly with it. Unthinkingly, I hauled off and slapped her face hard.

O sin of sins! The result of my spontaneous rebellion was predictable. I was dragged by the back of my shirt to the principal's office and then sent home in disgrace, never to darken the school's doors again. But a miracle happened. Miss O'Brien, who taught the other section of the same grade, offered to take me in the very next day. Suffused with deep gratitude, I transferred from hell to heaven.

Where did that unforgivable, unforgettable slap in my teacher's face come from? Surely, way down deep inside me was someone who would no longer accept to be treated in this manner. I'm only sorry it took two years of humiliation and ill treatment for my inner protector to surge up and demand respect.

However, the new freedom came at a price. From then on, even in the heaven of Miss O'Brien's class, I was subject, from time to time, to attacks of uncontrollable rage. They also erupted at home when my older brother cornered me to hold me down and tickle me. Something would snap inside and I'd fight like an animal for survival. So although my need for recognition was finally met, the reordering of my world was brought about by violence.

There was plenty of violence on the dirty New York street where we lived. Children from our tenements played and fought in endless permutations and combinations. My adventures with them only served to deepen my self-doubt since whatever game was going on out in the street, I was last to be picked when they chose up sides. In other words, I was a follower. In the game of Stink Bomb, for example, I trailed behind as older kids threw burning rolls of film into apartment house lobbies and ran away. Or, in Morningside Heights Park, which the black kids considered their territory, the older boys in our gang would throw light bulbs at their feet, which shattered like explosions. Surprisingly, though usually last to escape, I never got caught.

Movies were another source of violence. Saturdays, after we finished our chores and received our weekly allowance, my brother and I would spend all afternoon watching a double feature, news, cartoons and The Perils of Pauline, all for seven cents (a few years later it was raised to 11 cents). If you arrived in the middle of a good film and wanted to see it through again, you stayed on even longer.

Since World War II began a few months after we moved to New York, most of the movies I saw were full of thunder, bombing, torture and dead bodies. A few scenes are forever engraved in my mind. For example, in the final minutes of "Manila Calling," the last embattled American soldiers crouch under a table, radioing for help amid huge sounds of bombs that crash all around them, shaking their jungle shack. I can still hear their anguished voices repeatedly crying: "Manila calling, Manila calling." But there was no answer. Did the final explosion blow them up as the film ended or only create the impression that they were about to die? The soldiers' cries and the bomb-rocked scene are still with me, as alive as when I was 11 years old.

At some point, psychic self-protection must have set in because as an adult I refused to see war movies. I also began to peek at the end of every new book before taking it out of the library. That way, I could avoid sad stories in which someone died at the end. Only Beth's death in *Little Women* caught me unprepared. I steamed with outrage at having exposed myself unknowingly to more unbearable pain.

When I entered 7th grade, we moved from the Upper West Side to the East 70's and I changed schools. By the middle of my teenage years, the harsh experiences of childhood were forgotten, or at least buried below the mind. I became both a rebel and a hard worker. With "Don't tell me what to do!" and "I'll do it my way, thank you!" I met most forms of guidance. I wasn't popular, but I stood proudly on my own two feet. Only later, in discussing my childhood with a therapist, did I remember the taste of incoherent anger that could spew up in me like lava from a volcano's mouth.

My childhood experiences led me to build a fortress in myself against an untrustworthy world. Many people do it. What they don't realize—which I only became aware of in my 50's—is that it walls us in as well as keeps others out. When I began to scrutinize my inner defense system, I discovered that there inside, running the show, was an inner Tyrant. As I began to dialogue with him, I was relieved to learn that the harsh, endlessly critical voice inside my head was not, in fact, my own. He was neither my conscience nor my friend, but a persona figure who destroyed my confidence and often affected my relationships with others.

These dialogues took several forms. In the beginning, I conversed with the Tyrant and, soon after, with other persona figures when they appeared to my conscious mind. I called them my Cast of Characters. Later, I called on figures that appeared in my dreams, especially while the shock of the dream was still present as an emotional vibration. While the "experts" have very different opinions about the usefulness of dreams and what they mean, I find Edward C. Whitmont's poetic definition best fits my experience and understanding: "Like a flower or a hurricane or a human gesture, (the dream's) basic purpose is the manifestation and expression of this life force." (*Dreams: The Portal to the Source*, Whitmont & Perera)

At that time, many of my dreams circled around murderers and victims. For example: *A brilliant young student gets caught up in a murder. Then someone recognizes him so he has to kill him, too. A brilliant professor takes him home, thinking he can offer a better "argument" than murder. But the professor disappears. Will his wife be next? The dream becomes a horror tale in which the young man is forced to kill person after person so they won't find him out.*

"What's getting killed off in me?" I wondered and began a dialogue with the murderer

Why did you kill?
THEY WOULD HAVE EXPOSED ME.

What would have been exposed?
I'M NOT AS BRILLIANT AS THEY ALL THINK.

Why does that matter?
YOU ARE REALLY STUPID! I HAVE TO KEEP UP THE ILLUSION AND WIPE OUT ANYONE WHO FIGURES IT OUT.

What in me have you been killing?
YOU CLEARLY DON'T UNDERSTAND!

Can you explain anything of it to help me?
NOBODY MUST KNOW I'M JUST LIKE EVERYBODY ELSE!

That's how I first learned that an angry perfectionist inside me was killing off some other, gentler parts to maintain my defenses against the world. Another dream soon followed: *There's a powerful, nasty man who always has to get his own way. He has a slave who does all his work for him and has carried his burdens for so long they have grown into his back.*

So I asked the nasty man:

Why are you so mean?
YOU'VE GOT TO CUT CORNERS AND GO TO THE HEART OF THE MATTER.

But you seem to have no heart.
WHAT DO YOU KNOW? NOTHING!

I know what "nasty" and "mean" are and you've been called that. Why?
THIS IS STUPID. I CAN'T TALK WITH YOU BECAUSE YOU JUST DON'T KNOW ENOUGH!

Then I turned to the slave with the burdens tied to his back:
What do you carry that's so heavy?
THE WEIGHT OF A LIFETIME OF OBEDIENCE.

Obedience to what or to whom?
TO THE WRONG LEADER.

Can't you get away?
IT'S HARD. EASIER TO BECOME INVISIBLE ANY TIME I CAN.

But what if I need you to fight for me?
I'LL DO MY BEST BUT YOU HAVE TO HELP, TOO.

How can I help?
WAIT AND SEE.

This conversation left me shaken and confused. As Jung said, "An encounter with the unconscious is always a shock." If I was both the murderer and the slave, whom did I want to kill and what was I enslaved by? Although that was something I couldn't figure out, the complaints of the slave part pierced me. They forced me to admit to my tendency to become "invisible" in social situations when I didn't communicate honestly about my real feelings.

Confused or not, I would have to act on this new knowledge, to bring it into my daily life. That's an essential next step if you want to become free of the compulsive behavior of your complexes or personas. It's not enough just to notice them or even talk to them. As Jung pointed out, "I took great care to try to understand every single image, every item of my psychic inventory, and to classify them scientifically…and, above all, to realize them in actual life. That is what we usually neglect to do. We allow the images to rise up and maybe we wonder about them but…we do not take the trouble to understand them." (*MDR*)

Perhaps, like me, you armored yourself to keep hurt at a distance. It's natural for us to defend ourselves against a threatening world when we're young. But, as adults, we seldom need so much protection. What's more, as time goes by, keeping our defenses in place demands more and more energy from us. And we discover life is dull and lonely when we've cut ourselves off from feelings in order not to be hurt.

However, while we've probably outgrown the need for them, we remain imprisoned inside the armor we developed and the fortress we ourselves built—unless we become conscious of them. How to shed some of the defenses that are no longer needed? And why do we feel so threatened by change?

That's the rub! This experiment with dialogues is not a quick fix. Even when I became aware of my dilemma, it took years to break down the fortress walls so I could be more related to myself and more open to other people. Quite recently, the work of Jungian therapist Donald Kalsched, author of *The Inner World of Trauma*, cast further light on the psychological shackles I'd created for myself. You'll hear more about his findings in the next chapter.

THE PAST IS PRESENT IN YOU

Yes, you need to delve into past experiences to remember what happened long ago, and dialogue with yourself as a child. It may hurt. It may horrify. But you do it in the name of your present situation. What's important is to discover the ways in which those long ago experiences dominate your life right now. You may meet your childhood ghosts every day. (For more on ghosts, see Chapter 13)

FORGIVE THE WORLD FOR HAVING GIVEN YOU A HARD TIME

You may remember every second you suffered scorn, punishment or humiliation as if it were yesterday. But now it's time to let go of the anger that may surge up every time you think about it. Do you have a right to the rage you feel? Yes. But what's it doing to your present life? Do you continue to project that anger on other people? Are you highly sensitive to scorn? In my case, I saw that certain attitudes or energies coming from other people either evoked rage or completely undid me, rendering me helpless to respond. So best to let that anger float away down the river of your life.

GIVE UP THE BLAME GAME

It's hard to believe nobody's to blame for your harsh times, although even the bully was probably unable to help himself. Nevertheless, even if those who gave you a hard time were "bad to the bone," you still need to be free of them and their hidden power over your inner life. That was then, this is now. Move forward.

FORGIVE YOURSELF FOR NOT BEING A CONQUERING HERO

The fact that I didn't fight back, that I accepted to be attacked by my teacher and classmates for two hateful, agonizing years, calls up a sense of humiliation every time I think about it. Why didn't I punch back or walk out on them or pay no attention? Why did I let people who meant nothing to me hurt me so? The simple answer was hard to accept: Because I'm human. I'm part of society. I live in interaction with the people around me and want them to like me. We aren't born to fly solo through life. We need relationships with others as well as a good feeling about ourselves.

FIND OUT WHAT YOU NEED TO KNOW
You want to understand what happened, why it happened and how it affected your psyche and created your attitude toward life. That way, your reaction will cease to be a negative backlash you don't even see coming. Begin by calling to mind some past incident. Bring it to life. Zoom in on it until your emotional reactions get stirred, but hold onto your wish to understand so you don't get caught up in them.

STAY IN CHARGE
That means you need to stay related to yourself, here and now, as an adult, while you accept to be inundated by the suffering and humiliation of the child you once were. If you have the courage to do that, you can actually help the inner child leave it behind. You can even free your family and other people still in your life from the attitudes that surged out of your past psychic prison.

CONSULT YOUR INNER GUIDE
As the reactions to those long-ago moments begin to spread through you, heating up your capillaries, inducing a ringing in your ears or even outright blind rage, stay in the pilot's seat and maneuver through the storm. You may never know what caused others to treat you so badly. So give it up. Rather, ask your inner guide why you responded the way you did.

FACE UP TO YOUR OWN REALITY
Are you distrustful, like my mother, or suspicious of friendliness in others? Perhaps you feel every gift disguises a demand, every gesture a possible blow, as I did. Or perhaps you condemn yourself for always being in the wrong. It's time to connect the dots, wherever they may lead you.

TALK IT OUT
Find the questions that take you a step nearer to understanding what was going on at that time. Then ask the angry maniac inside or the cowering slave (or whoever else appears) your burning questions. Listen to what they have to say and write it down. You may not understand it now, but when you read it again later on a little light may dawn.

"THE WAY IN IS THE WAY OUT"
In his Four Quartets, T. S. Eliot documented many aspects of our dilemma and offered us new ways of looking at them. Don't justify yourself or accuse yourself. Don't judge the old emotional reactions as you try to stay on an even keel. However difficult it is, a dialogue with part of yourself that was constellated when you re-lived an event will throw light on similar dynamics that are still in play. You may not know what they are but you can begin to explore their effect on your present life. If you need help with this daunting task, you may want to consult a therapist.

Five: The "Protector" Becomes a "Persecutor"

"Once the inner psychological protector has been constellated it will fight for its life, and it will do all it can to prevent possible re-traumatisation. In doing so, it becomes an unwitting and violent inner persecutor, inflicting more pain, trauma and abuse upon oneself than the original trauma, and external world, ever did...In short...the self-defense system ends by turning against the very person it is supposed to be protecting."
Donald Kalsched, *Caduceus Journal*, 2006

Self-protection is one of our deepest instincts. When a child goes through a traumatic experience, the sensitive core originally open to the world moves into hiding, deep within the being. An internal protector is constellated to prevent that core from being subjected to indignity or desecration.

Dr. Kalsched, author of *The Inner World of Trauma*, believes that this Protector, who guards us from intolerable pain, later turns into a Persecutor. The same energy that defended the helpless child from unbearable suffering interferes with growth long after protection is needed. Here's how he explains it: "The essence of the child—the creative, relational, authentic innocent spark of life...goes into hiding, deep in the unconscious. At the same time, another part of the child's psyche grows up prematurely and becomes a rigid psychological defence system that will use whatever means it can to protect that innocent essence and keep it hidden out of harm's way."

While the original splitting was perhaps necessary to save the child from "psychological annihilation," she later turns her natural anger inward, against herself. This creates a "self-blaming system that splits the psyche between a supposedly inadequate inner child and the critical inner protector." Like an autoimmune disease in which the killer cells attack healthy tissue as if they were intruder cells, the system turns against the person it's trying to protect. As a result, the child may grow up hating both her body and her emotions.

This self-blaming system isn't limited to cases of severe trauma. Kalsched says a protector/persecutor lives in every one of us to some degree: "We all grow up in a home, or society, where only parts of ourselves have been allowed to blossom," he points out, "while other parts that were unacceptable have been locked away in a hidden recess of our being. Few of us move into the second half of life having lived the first half in an environment where we were fully seen, mirrored, validated and allowed to live. So we are all somewhat injured, and we will all have constellated some kind of Protector/Persecutor system. If you haven't suffered 'trauma' as a child, the system will not be so extreme, primitive or rigid, but it will still limit your potential and prevent you from being fully alive."

In spite of family pressures described in previous chapters, I'd been a well-loved child. What wounding had awakened the protector/persecutor in me? Fast-forward from the happy eight-year-old, who loved the country, to the nine-year-old whose solid roots had been torn from that fertile ground and replanted in a tenement on a smelly New York street. Then enter the Wicked Witch, in the form of my 4th and 5th grade teacher and the cruel children who made my life a living hell.

For two years I absorbed Miss P.'s psychological abuse, until the dam broke and I slapped her. Bad girl, yes. But good for me! However, from then on I was subject to bouts of violent rage. It had become unbearable to be accused of even the smallest infraction or physically imprisoned in any way. Now I recognize this as the birth of an anguished, trapped feeling that became familiar in later years as: There's NO WAY OUT! (See Chapter 17). If your past holds a similar situation, a dialogue with your Persecutor could be life-restoring. When I did it, I received harsh but enlightening answers and learned what a passive child I'd been, offering myself indiscriminately to be liked and expecting approval in return.

When the protector appears, says Kalsched, it will do anything to prevent a repeat of the original trauma. It may morph into a murderer, a devil or a terrorist. From then on, the closed system remains poised at the level of the original trauma, even though the child grows up and develops other means to defend itself. The essence of its being has been locked away, "safe" forever, along with the primary energy it contains, leaving the human being with a "survival self-care system (that) says 'no' to life."

Even if you know all this, how do you recognize the Persecutor in yourself? According to Kalsched, it's the voice that says "you aren't loveable so better not allow yourself to love" or, as in my mother's case, "don't trust anyone, no matter how nice they seem." When you hear these or similar voices, start a conversation. It might provide unexpected insight.

In my own case, awareness of the inner Persecutor began to unfold after the breakup of my family and my return to New York from Peru. At that time I lived every day with pain, guilt and a sense of my own inadequacy. Haunting one-sentence messages at the close of dreams I couldn't recall began to accuse me, enigmatic phrases that often went right to the heart of what I needed to see or do. The first of these "one-liners" was: *TEAR THEM DOWN AFTER A LIFETIME OF PUTTING UP WALLS.*

Although I didn't "get it" right away, the cryptic message indicated it was time to break down my protective fortress and open up to life. A few nights later, another one-liner called attention to my tendency to help others whatever the cost. I'd thought of it as positively virtuous. But the scornful tone of the accusation signaled an entirely different meaning: *ANY PRICE THAT HAS TO BE PAID—YOU'RE AVAILABLE TO PAY IT!*

Startled, I asked myself, "Is that true? Does my perception of someone's need bring me full speed ahead, all systems go, to help, save, pay?" As if in answer to my question, the image of a fish came to mind, darting blindly at a temptingly baited hook. I wrote in my journal: *So that's how much I'm impelled to help when someone seems needy! Could it be I who need help? If so, why do I respond so urgently to others' needs and put my own needs last? Is it a form of punishing myself, this readiness to "pay any price?"*

Who are you, who says I deserve to pay and pay hard?
TAKE THAT AND THAT AND THAT!   I'LL SHOW YOU WHAT PAYING IS TILL IT COMES OUT OF YOUR EARS! YOU'LL BE SORRY YOU OFFERED!

So who are you, who says "take that and that and that?"
WHAT DO YOU CARE?

I care. That's why I'm asking.   I need to understand why you want to hurt me so.
KILL THE BIRD!

You want to kill the bird, beat the gentle, crush the frightened, the meek, and trample on the bud just opening. Why?
BECAUSE IT HURTS, HURTS, HURTS!   IT HURTS SO MUCH TO LISTEN, TO LOVE, TO CARE FOR, TO CHERISH. IT HURTS AND HURTS AND HURTS. SO WHY NOT CRUSH IT BEFORE IT GETS A CHANCE TO HURT?

I wish I knew the answer to that. I feel it, too. To open oneself again and again to love and receive a kick in the shin, a punch in the belly, a stab in the back...I guess I have to trust the wise people who tell me to go on, not to give up.   But sometimes I wonder if my heart will break...

THAT'S WHY IT'S BETTER TO HAVE NO HEART.   THEN NOTHING WILL BREAK. NOTHING WILL BE HURT. TEAR OUT YOUR HEART AND THROW IT AWAY!

I don't know what to say.   But I do believe a heart can break, and my heart has seemed to hurt so much it couldn't go on beating and sustaining life.

AND YET YOU OPEN YOURSELF UP TO MORE OF THE SAME AGAIN AND AGAIN.   WHAT ARE YOU, A MASOCHIST?

Maybe I am. I only know more and more that I can't be any different from what I am. So I guess I just have to learn to bear it.

THAT MAY BE YOUR IDEA OF FUN BUT IT'S NOT MINE!

That was my first conversation with my inner Tyrant. It left me breathless, wondering what was going on. Yet, while I reeled from the unpleasant accusations, the exchange provided useful information that took me by surprise. For example, I didn't think of myself as being in pain until the Tyrant pointed it out. My conscious attitude to the blows I'd received was, "That's life. Suck it up!" I was also shocked that some unknown part of me didn't go along with the self-sacrifice I considered a virtue.

Shortly after that exchange, I began to notice unpleasant, self-destructive fantasies. For example, a few mornings later I had trouble getting out of bed although I had to be at the office early for an important meeting. Lying there, listening to the clock tick away the time, I fantasized taking a gun and shooting myself. It wasn't suicide, but punishment. As if that's what I deserved. "Wow!" I thought, "I'm up against something cold, hard, really nasty."

A few nights later, another one-liner was fired at me: *YOU MAKE A MESS OF THE BEST!* I took it as a scolding, but what had I done wrong? The next day was New Years Eve, feeling desperate, I begged my inner world to explain:

What do you wish for me?
THAT YOU FIND YOUR OWN WAY, NOT JUST FORCED TO PLEASE, BUT ABLE TO BE YOURSELF, COME TO DECISIONS BY YOURSELF. BUT TO DO THIS YOU MUST BE PRESENT, SO I GUESS I WISH FOR YOU TO BE "HERE" MORE OFTEN, TO LIVE MORE FREQUENTLY FROM YOURSELF, RATHER THAN FROM WHAT OTHERS LIKE OR THINK IS "RIGHT." GOOD LUCK!

"Hey," I thought. "This is a completely different voice. These inner messages aren't always negative, forever on the attack!" I wondered whether my dialogues had constellated an Inner Guide, someone above the fray.

EXAMINE THE WALLS OF THE FORTRESS YOU'VE BUILT
We protect ourselves in many ways, some of them quite unconscious. The walls we built up in childhood or in extreme situations may have been necessary at the time, but they keep life out as well as maintain our illusion that we are safe inside. What's more, as James Hollis pointed out in What Matters Most, *"The more we invest in building a fortress to protect ourselves from life, the less secure we feel."*

DO YOUR WALLS KEEP OTHERS OUT?
What word best describes your attitude in your most recent encounter with a stranger? Were you cool, suspicious, condescending, helpless, apologetic? Try to take a step back into that moment and connect it with similar moments. Can you scope out your general attitude and the story you weave to explain it?

WHAT ARE YOUR WALLS MADE OF?
Some may be impenetrable stone, like the castle that protected Sleeping Beauty. But others may be paper thin and easier to break through. Analyze the quality of your interactions with others. When do you try to please and why? If you notice you've suddenly cut someone off, ask yourself, "What triggered that reaction?" For example, some of us hold others off by exuding warmth ("How <u>are</u> you, darling?"), others by freezing up ("Don't tread on me!").

BY CLOSING OTHERS OUT, YOU CLOSE YOURSELF OUT AS WELL
Relationship is a two-way street between me and other people, but also between me and my inner self. So if I can't relate easily to others, I probably have trouble relating to myself. If that's true for you, you might want to uncover the history behind your current defenses. Why did you build them up in just that particular way? How do you treat yourself in comparison with how you treat others? In what ways do you refuse yourself the help, the care, the benefit of the doubt you offer them?

IS YOUR FIRST RESPONSE FIGHT OR FLIGHT?
It's sometimes said that each of us acts out either as an attacker or a victim. Which are you? When someone accuses you of something, do you fight back right away or nurse your wounds, feeling hurt and badly treated? When faced with a sudden confrontation, is your first move to face up to it or do you leave the room? Don't think of your responses as 'right' or 'wrong,' rather that we discover more about ourselves if we can answer these questions.

GET TO KNOW YOUR PERSECUTOR
What do you accuse yourself of? An exchange with your inner Tyrant can be highly productive. But keep in mind that just because he berates you all day long doesn't mean he's right. If he's like mine, he'll find accusations to suit every occasion. And you've probably heard them since childhood.

TAKE DICTATION FROM HIM
Listen attentively. These inner comments and their "tone of voice" are important. Write them down as soon as possible. Then you can open a dialogue. Ask him why he's making these accusations or calling you these names. He may give you a nasty answer like those I received, but you're sure to learn something about yourself, whatever he says.

OUR MOODS THEMSELVES CAN BE TYRANNICAL
As we study these voices in ourselves, we can uncover many subtle forms of tyranny. For example, self-pity is another example of self-persecution. Whenever my inner world shrinks into "poor little me," I remind myself of a Chippewa saying: "Sometimes I go about pitying myself. And all the time I am carried on great winds across the sky."

REMEMBERING BRINGS BOTH PAIN AND HEALING
According to Kalsched: "The divine often comes to us through the broken places, through those split off and shameful places which are almost always traumatic. When the exiled parts of us are remembered, re-membered, recollected and re-collected, and we can welcome them into our lives, there is profound healing."

Six: The Time of the Hero

"We have not even to face the adventure alone, for the heroes of all time have gone before us: the labyrinth is thoroughly known; we have only to follow the thread of the hero path. And where we had thought to find an abomination, we shall find a god, and where we had thought to slay another, we shall slay ourselves. Where we had thought to travel outward, we shall come to the center of our own existence, and where we had thought to be alone, we shall be with all the World."

Joseph Campbell, *The Hero with a Thousand Faces*

Childhood and youth are the time of the hero. Young and vulnerable, we need someone to protect us from the early blows of life. If our parents or teachers can't do that, we'll invent hero companions, a super-person or a powerful animal to defend us. Perhaps that's why action comics are so successful.

No matter whether the perceived attack comes from family members, schoolmates or the world, it will sooner or later constellate an inner hero, a persona who can handle it all. As we grow up we unconsciously bring our inner hero along to help us meet new challenges, succeed at school, forge a career, raise a family, seek success in the outer world.

My own favorite imaginary playmates were Batman, Superman and the fairies. The first two were amazingly strong and the latter protected me with their magical powers. When I outgrew them, a Handsome Hero began to inhabit my dreams and fantasies. In my adolescent years, he was often a wounded pilot, shot down by the enemy. It was my job to care for him and protect him from discovery.

In college and on the job, I fought hard to succeed. What pushed me onward? Why did I have to prove myself again and again? In his book, *The Soul's Code*, psychologist James Hillman says we each have our own myth. So we live not only heroically, but often within a whole mythology. In order to find happiness and meaning in the second half of life, we need to rediscover our myth. Do we live by it or oppose it at every turn? In a recent lecture, Hillman added: "Once you know the mythical pattern of your suffering, you are halfway on the road to relief." (Jungian Psychoanalytic Association, 2008)

Some myths offer clear messages; others fascinate us without our knowing why. For example, take the great Hero story of Parsival, the purest of King Arthur's knights. Tales of knights who sought perfection in action fit my personal ethos since perfection was central to my sense of Self.

But the tale includes a warning: perhaps Parsival was too pure, too perfect. He went all over the kingdom in search of the Holy Grail, the vessel in which Christ's blood had supposedly been kept. But, when he neared his goal, he got lost. From then on he had to depend on his horse to lead him because his mind didn't know enough to get him there. That's the message perfectionists don't hear: our heart and body are indispensable to lead us to that new place.

And what did he find? A wounded king. Perhaps we are all kings and queens of an inner country, a place that is truly our own, with which we lost touch long ago. Wounded and in need of help like the Fisher King, we need to ask the right questions. Parsival forgot to ask, which is why he woke up next morning in a barren desert, with castle, king and opportunity lost forever. The question I had failed to ask during my years of pain and guilt, was: "What do my wounds serve?"

In any case, I rediscovered my personal myth during my plunge into Jungian studies. Still vibrant, it resurfaced suddenly when I confronted different sides of myself. As a teenager, I'd found a book on my mother's shelf called *OM: The Secret of Ahbor Valley*, an East Indian spy-thriller by Talbot Mundy. It told of a mysterious valley beyond the great mountains in Northern India, guarded by a savage tribe whose members killed anyone hardy enough to survive the terrible climb over the Himalayas.

In this valley lived the Masters, legendary wise men who, since the dawn of time, have kept alive the ancient knowledge that can save civilization whenever it is bent on destroying itself. At the heart of this domain of higher beings was a Great Jade, a huge stone of extraordinary properties, set in the ground at the center of a circular gathering place. Those who had the courage to look into its depths would see themselves reflected. But not many people want to see all they really are. Any who looked would first see to their horror all they couldn't bear to admit to themselves: their faults, their lies, their devils, their wickedness. Only a few pure mortals who hadn't fainted away from the shock of that first glance could discern their potentiality, like a vision deep in the stone: the essence of who they are.

The Priestess was the only native to the valley apart from the savage tribe, for the Masters had learned the secret of perpetual life and lived there for thousands of years. She was born as her father and mother were dying, he of wounds from the attack of a band of robbers as they fled over the mountains; she in childbirth, exhausted by the journey. The savage guards brought the newborn to the Masters, who decided to educate her, untouched by the destructive influences of mankind, from birth to perfection as an adult. They would share with her their secret knowledge, then send her out into the world to propagate their understanding and awaken a new vision of human possibility. To accompany her, they brought some twenty unwanted orphans into the valley, girl babies they collected from all over the world.

The children developed into extraordinary young women, icons of purity, intelligence and multifaceted talents. They were all that I longed to be: true, honest, discriminating, highly educated, talented in the arts and languages. Part of their education had been the ritual obligation to look periodically into the stone, and correct any faults they saw in themselves. However, even though they were close to perfection, these girls were forced to look into the stone at night, by the gentle light of the moon, so as not to be overwhelmed. Only their leader, the girl born in the valley, high priestess to the stone, could look into it in the full light of day.

Although I loved this book and read it many times as a teenager, I forgot all about it when I went to college. Later, as a stressed-out reporter at *Time*, or a pressured wife and mother raising a family and running a school in Peru, I was too busy to think about heroines. Instead, I lived my own heroic story in what I thought of as the Real World: star reporter, wife and mother, school director, President of the Green Cross and wife of the governor of a huge jungle province in Peru. If fantasies continued to bubble in my unconscious, I never noticed them.

But, when my marriage of 18 years foundered, I fled back to New York to become a single working mother with three children. Under attack from both physical and psychic pain, I cried out: "What have I done wrong?" Was this a personal punishment for having left my marriage and broken up my family? I confided my misery to a friend who suggested I write down my dreams. "What dreams?" I asked, proud to affirm I seldom dreamed—so concentrated was I on developing greater consciousness!

As if on cue, nightmares began to jolt me awake in the dead night hours. A door cracked opened into alien territory as a multitude of heroes and bad guys, hostile tyrants and deadly spies made me sweat with fear or tremble with cold. Shakily, I'd write the dreams down then and there because by morning they were erased from my conscious mind. My therapist later explained to me that this was because there was almost no communication between my conscious life and the unconscious world within.

From Jung's point of view, every character in a dream represents some aspect of our inner world. Then why were they so

violent, so extreme? Why were there so many enemies out to get
the good guys? Why these endless battles and wars? Tyrants,
torturers and terrorists wielded uncanny power over heroes or small
bands of people trying to escape. The heroes always faced
impossible odds, and though they worked their hearts out and never
gave up the fight, they always got captured, tortured or killed in the
end. Yet it never occurred to me that the nightmares might be
related to my struggle to lead three lives as a single parent, a
daughter caring for elderly parents, and a journalist trying to keep
my head and bank account above water.

In his autobiography, Jung writes: "In the final analysis the
decisive factor is always consciousness, which can understand the
manifestations of the unconscious and take up a position toward
them." (*MDR*) That sounded fine, but what position could I
possibly take, adrift among threatening psychic forces?

One early dream stands out: *A Christ-like figure tries to
escape from a low, dome-like structure. He negotiates the deep
moat that surrounds it and is climbing up the other side, giving
hope to the rest of us that at least the best of us would get away.
But he's caught and led back across the bridge to the dome in
heavy chains, a long line of guards on either side of him. They step
slowly to the measured rhythm of beautiful funeral music sung by a
choir.*

The message was clear: No one can escape, not even the
most spiritual person. There is NO WAY OUT. The next day a
sense of deep mourning accompanied me everywhere I went.
Although the feeling gradually faded, the same message wove itself
into my days and nights for months, even years: there was No Way
Out.

These dream stories, sometimes as simplistic as the comics
I'd read as a child, made no sense to my daytime mind. Even so, I
couldn't shake off the foreboding they produced, a dark shadow on
my conscious life. For example, one night a dream-cop walked into
the room at the last minute (to my great relief), to save us good

guys from being slaughtered. Was he my hero? I watched with satisfaction as he shot the gangsters who were about to kill us. But then—to my horror—he turned his gun towards me and coldly shot me right between the eyes.

Shocked awake, I couldn't sleep for hours. When my rapid heartbeat quieted, I tried to figure out the new message: were the cops in me not to be trusted any more than the criminals? A policeman shoots me in the forehead when I tell him about a criminal, although I expected him to turn his gun on the bad guy. A criminal shoots me in the belly, just as I thought I'd convinced him I wouldn't betray him. Tyrants, assassins, police, criminals, all were telling me something important, but I just wasn't getting it.

It was months before the light dawned. My own naiveté was getting shot both by The Policeman, who represented one side of me, and The Criminal, who represented another. "If neither of them is the real 'me,' who are they?" I wondered. The Policeman kept things under control, within the law, pursued the bad guys and put them in jail. That was reasonable. But where, in the Good Girl that I was, did a Criminal hide? Was my crime that I hid my real feelings from myself? Did the dreams suggest I should express them more? Or was I supposed to "make nice" because I'd get shot if I strayed from the Good Girl path?

In either case, the theme was betrayal. Who was betrayed and by what actions of mine? How did I betray myself? And who was the innocent bystander always under attack, shocked by what she never expected to happen to her? Ahah! Was being 'shot' a play on the word shocked?

Even as my mind bounced these thoughts around during the day, my nights became more fearsome. I took to staying up later and later, in the hope that I'd be too tired to dream. Could it get any worse? Yes! Finally the Nazi appeared, a sadist who enjoyed torture for its own sake. He smiled as he twisted his knife in the wounds of his prisoners. And the worst moment of all, a sharp stab in my heart, came when I was forced to accept that the sadistic torturer must live somewhere in me! However, once I was able to assimilate that fact, he never visited me again.

As the hero dreams continued, they developed a new twist which made it clear that I couldn't even trust my savior! *A Viking ship, with a great female figure carved on the bowsprit, moves implacably through the ocean waves. The handsome hero-captain, poised like a statue on the bow, looks into the far distance, quite unaware that I'm swimming in the water just below him, about to be crushed by the hull. I shout and shout at him as the enormous ship plows on its course, but the captain takes no notice of what's right in front of him.*

This was a terrifying wake-up call. My Hero, my Ideal Man, had come to rescue me, yet he was unmindful of my existence far below, drowning in the waters of the unconscious. Was the dream saying the Hero persona in me didn't see what was right in front of me? I examined my everyday situation. To dream of heroes was one thing. That was often exciting. But how did I act out the hero in real life? The answer wasn't far away. One look into my past revealed how I'd lived the part of the Hero many times: the *Time* reporter who got the interview no one else could; the wife and mother who kept the family together in Peru in spite of poverty and galloping inflation. (At one point I held four jobs a day as I ferried children to my school from their scattered homes, ran the school all morning, then taught English to private students in the afternoons and Tai Chi classes in the evenings.)

My epic drama had continued on my return to New York, where I held down demanding editorial jobs, then rushed home to prepare a "well-balanced meal" in my attempt to fill my role of Good Mother. Even as I recovered from two surgeries, or fought the fatigue of cholestatic hepatitis and daily reflux pain, I kept on going. My life as a heroic drama had its price: a gut reaction with indigestion and nightmares.

I tried to make sense of all this. On the one hand, I figured, it's in the nature of the hero to insist he will forge ahead against all odds. As Robert Johnson writes in *Balancing Heaven and Earth*, "This is an appropriate role for the ego—to provide courage and determination. Properly applied, the ego is used not for decision-making but as the eyes and ears of God—collecting information, marshalling energies for the task at hand, providing discipline and courage. The heroic ego has an important task, but clearly it must rely upon help from others."

On the other hand, everything I did had the unpleasant taste of an ordeal—even the simplest things. It was as if I had to prove myself, over and over. However, the heroic drama I lived each day couldn't go on forever. For one thing, my defenses were breaking down. I no longer wore the heavy coat of internal armor that had protected me for years. For another, my illnesses cried out to me that something was very wrong.

One of my last hero dreams was especially violent: *a hero stands out bravely against a host of bad guys who want to make him pay (for what?). But army, police and all kinds of authority are against him and he gets beaten up a lot. He's hardy and exchanges light quips with lawmen but the menace of a whole law enforcement organization often overcomes him. Not yet cowed by them, he's still a hero, but how long can he hold out against their amassed power?*

The question rang in my ears. How long could he/I go on this way? And what was it all for? To my surprise, the very next night the Hero turned to me, his dream companion, and said he planned to retire soon. He was going to give up his exciting job and work full time in a gas station at the headquarters of a desert police outfit. But what was I supposed to figure out from that message? If I gave up driving myself heroically onward and upward, who would get things done?

A few nights later a strange new figure appeared: *Several of us are in a desert below a mountain, accompanied by a small man dressed for an African safari—a caricature of an English explorer, helmet and all. Suddenly a giant comes down from the mountain and gestures for us to follow him. The Explorer tries to defend us against this huge, hairy, possibly savage being, but the massive giant lifts him high in his arms, then stretches him out on the ground, tying his four limbs to stakes and leaving him spread-eagled on the sand.*

Why had the Explorer who tried to be a hero been turned into a comic figure, unmanned, exposed, stretched out helpless and unconscious? Dismayed, I asked the giant:

Wild man from the mountain…who are you? Why have you come down from the hills?
DON'T GIVE ME WORDS.

How can we converse? I need to know what you want of me.
Silence.

Are you here to help?
I AM HELP!

Then I'll try to listen for your presence. You are so huge, it's a bit scary.
Silence.

Why did you lay out the Explorer that way?
IT WAS TIME FOR HIM TO GO.

Am I to enter your world or will you enter mine?
A long silence...then: LISTEN TO ANOTHER VOICE.

I wrote in my journal: *YES! I want to listen to another voice. I don't want to live by the old rules of crime and punishment. I will no longer live by DOING THE RIGHT THING according to some hyper-conscientious paradigm. No! And to live consciously means I must be present to what I don't want as well as what I want. I wish to be present to my life, in contact with my SELF—the lover, the carer, the attentive one in me.*

FIND YOUR OWN PERSONAL MYTH

One way is to look for an actual legend or fairytale you've remembered since childhood, a story you cherished or lived out or perhaps even denied in yourself, affirming its opposite. To detect it, study the longings and gut reactions that have erupted in you ever since your own personal tale on earth began. Whether we are aware of it or not as adults, this hidden fantasy is still close to our hearts and entwined in our unconscious drives.

IT'S STORY TIME

Find a comfortable chair, close your eyes and let your mind wander back to the favorite stories of your childhood, be they fairytales, myths or comics. One or another of them made a place for itself in your heart. Did you identify yourself with Cinderella or Hercules? Sleeping Beauty or the Handsome Prince? King Arthur, the Ice Maiden, Superman? Or maybe a dwarf like Rumpelstiltskin tickled your fancy, or a wise wizard like Merlin, or the cat who looked at a king.

YOUR CHILDREN CAN HELP
If you find this exercise difficult, go to your children's bookshelves. Hopefully, you read them stories all the time. If nothing comes up, ask your kids what stories they like best. They're still plugged into the magical world of myth and fable. Or if there are no children around to consult, visit your local library and browse the children's section until you find something that triggers your fascination.

WHICH TALES OR CHARACTERS TOUCHED YOU TO THE CORE?
As you re-live the experiences in the story that grabs you most, imagine yourself in one or another of the parts. The role of the hero or heroine usually satisfies a taste for adventure but you can also connect with the life of other characters, even animals, in the drama. Where does a story resemble your story? How do the characters manage their problems?

GENTLY DOES IT
Don't jump too fast into these roles; rather, let them come alive in you. Go carefully at first, as if you were talking to a shy child who might be frightened, and whom you're trying to get to know. Easy questions; delicate curiosity. Don't be surprised if it's hard to get started. Give it time. Listen.

REVISIT YOUR REAL-LIFE HEROES
Sometimes it's easier to begin with real people you admire. Ask yourself, what do you like about them and why? How might you wish to be like them? What traits or powers do you wish you had? A larger-than-life enemy can also throw light on your study. What can't you stand about him or her? Gather information like the scientist we spoke of earlier, objectively collecting data.

MEET ONE OF THESE CHARACTERS FACE TO FACE
Now choose a figure you'd like to know more about, sit quietly and visualize him or her or it. Then open a dialogue. What does the hero want to tell you? Or the dragon he conquered, or the rescued

princess?

REAL PEOPLE LIVE IN YOU, TOO
You can hold inner conversations with real people you admire as well as fantasy figures, because they've already made a place for themselves in you. Like your parents and siblings, they live on in your inner life in some way. What advice would your great grandmother give you, or Abraham Lincoln, or Gandhi, or Martha Washington, or the first man to climb Everest, or even the man who never made it all the way?

WRITE IT ALL DOWN
Write about your heroes, real or imagined, and try to be specific about what attracts you to them. Note down the fragments of stories, myths and fantasies that fascinate or repel you. Describe your emotions about them. This is part of your work to uncover your own inner life.

LET IT GO, THEN TAKE IT UP AGAIN
When you begin these experiments they may produce powerful reactions. Once you've gathered the data, you may want to put it aside to re-read another day, in quiet circumstances. Don't give up. Just wait a day or two and read your notes again. New understandings, even "ahas!" may reward you. It's like listening to a new language.

Seven: "Addiction to Perfection"

"Where perfection is worshipped in consciousness, imperfection is magnetic in the unconscious. Splitting light from dark denies human wholeness."

Marion Woodman, *The Ravaged Bridegroom*

It wasn't till midlife, when I read Marion Woodman's *Addiction to Perfection*, that I began to suspect my wish to be perfect might be an aspect of my Inner Tyrant. Until then, I thought whatever in me sought to do and be the very best at everything was my Inner Guide. I had confused the Perfectionist with the Seeker.

There's a passionate Seeker in each of us. Whether we're conscious of it or not, we all long for some kind of fulfillment: fame or family, union with God or power over others, money, success, spiritual development, payback. My inmost desire had always been to find "the true Truth," although I'm not sure what I meant by that. A religious child, I dedicated much of my first two decades to pleasing God and Mother. That included a free use of prayer, primarily for my own ends. (For example, I often prayed for the Brooklyn Dodgers to win, as I huddled over my radio late into the night.)

You could say I was born into seeking, since my parents were students of a system of ideas taught by G. I. Gurdjieff about inner development through work on oneself. In fact, I first learned that we all harbor an inner Tyrant from his magnum opus, *Beelzebub's Tales to His Grandson*, where he wrote: "Jesus Christ and all the other prophets sent from Above spoke of the death which might occur even during life…the death of that 'Tyrant' from whom proceeds our slavery in this life…"

The Gurdjieff Work was, and continues to be, a major source of meaning and direction in my life. It has clarified my studies of Christianity, Hinduism, Buddhism, Judaism, Taoism and Zen. (A detailed account of Gurdjieff's "work in life" can be found in the first chapter of my book, *The Practice of Presence: Five Paths for Daily Life*.)

Gurdjieff came to New York when I was 15. I attended his classes of sacred dances—strange and wonderful movement exercises he'd brought back from travels in the East. They forced me to concentrate every ounce of my attention to combine the unusual rhythms and synchronize the head, arm, leg and foot positions. Twice a week, I'd finish my homework early and find my way by bus to Carnegie Hall Studios. For the rest of the evening I vibrated with energy and an acute awareness of life.

While I was in college, I began to meditate every morning. Over time, that brought me intermittent but extraordinary states of clarity and peace. Wonderful! Naturally, I wanted more of them! I ached to be the Perfect Seeker and arrive at new heights of spiritual experience but success always seemed just beyond my grasp.

Later, as a *Time* reporter, I sought perfection in action: to be the best at whatever I did. But after several intense years, life lost its special savor. I returned from my brother's wedding depressed. He'd married Mrs. Wonderful. I'd been looking for Mr. Knight in Shining Armor, or maybe for me it was Mr. Wise Man, but would I ever find him?

In the end, I didn't find Mr. Right, just Mr. the man I married. While God or Truth or spiritual experiences visited me from time to time, they certainly weren't available on demand. Perhaps I wasn't working at it hard enough, I thought, so I drove myself to be more conscious, more present, more helpful to others. In other words, more perfect!

When, in midlife, I began to reexamine what I was working so hard to achieve, I was forced to confront my longing for states of intense awareness. Was this "purest" desire of my inner life only a mythical experience? Or—more horrifying thought—was I simply in search of an adrenaline rush? How did a sense of inner presence differ from the excited awareness of a reporter on difficult interviews or the challenge to meet the deadline of a big story? Or later, as wife and mother, when I faced family emergencies in Peru with all the strength and intelligence I could muster, while running a school or living in the jungle? Could I have somehow confused life energy with the more subtle sense of vitality that is a gift of spiritual experience?

I was forced to reexamine my goals. Surely I'd imagined myself a modern member of Gurdjieff's Seekers of Truth, the band of adventurers he wrote about in his book, *Meetings with Remarkable Men*. But suddenly my yearnings seemed fantastic, and I a fool to have ventured so far from my own reality. Marion Woodman's call to "live within the limitations that make my life my own" (*Bone: Dying Into Life*) pierced my heart.

Surely it was time to give up dreams of spiritual ascension and find my feet here on solid earth! Determined to sacrifice my fantasy in the fires of a new beginning, I asked myself, "What do I really want?" Lightning fast came the answer: *to be loving, attentive, centered in my own presence; clear-thinking, authentic, spontaneous and unpretentious*. Yeow! How mythical was that!

Not surprisingly, this catalogue of coveted desires was swiftly followed by the scathing voice of the Tyrant: *WHO DO YOU THINK YOU ARE? YOU WORM IN SHEEP'S CLOTHING!*

To dodge his now-familiar attack, I called desperately for help: *How can I escape the attack of this Terrorist each time I discover something new about myself?* And to my amazement, there was an answer from another part of my forest of personas:

STOP FOLLOWING AN IDEAL WAY OF BEING. IT LEADS YOU TO ACCUSE YOURSELF. WHY DO YOU ATTACK YOUR WEAKNESS, CALL YOURSELF NAMES, SAY "I'VE FAILED AGAIN?"

It just seems I'm always off-base.

YOU MUST CARE FOR THIS CONFUSED PART. WHAT DOES IT NEED? BE AUTHENTIC, BUT NOT CONTROLLING.
But I'm afraid to give up control, because then where will I find the authority?

IT WOULD BE MORE HELPFUL TO NOTICE WHERE THE AUTHORITY ISN'T. WHY DO YOU FIND SAFETY AND APPROVAL ONLY IN "DOING," IN CHECKING ACCOMPLISHMENTS OFF YOUR DAILY LIST?
O.K. I admit that's how I live. But what can I do about it?

PRACTICE BEING YOURSELF, NOT YOUR IDEAL. LISTEN TO YOURSELF AND YOUR NEEDS AND RESPOND TO THEM.
But if I do that how can I guarantee I'll get everything done that needs to be done?

THAT'S THE WORK OF A LIFETIME.
        In spite of this good advice, the fight for supremacy between The Tyrannical Judge, the Frightened Child and the Perfectionist continued. To make matters worse, suddenly, one morning as I meditated a plaintive voice cried out: *I DON'T WANT TO BE ME. I WANT TO BE YOU!*
        This is terrible! I wrote in my journal. *I don't want to be who I am! I don't even like myself! The Perfectionist rejects what's partial, inadequate, confused, imperfect and decaying. But that's me!*
        I consulted my wise mother: "How can I find a relationship with God," I asked her. "Surely I need to become someone better!" "God isn't someone else," she replied. "As for trying to be 'better,' we need to see ourselves, not indulge in advanced surgery by

cutting off the parts we don't like." Her words shook me up. The downside of longing for perfection is that there's no room for a real person! How to be more deeply myself?

If your experience is in any way related to mine, you'll need to accept what I finally had to assimilate: the Perfectionist isn't an ideal at all. She's just another Terrorist! What's more, she and the Tyrant are in cahoots. He criticizes every move we make; she's got us in her torturing grip. *"**YOU'LL NEVER SUCCEED**,"* they both assure us. So we feel dejected and give up trying.

However, as soon as we question their authority, new discoveries await. I saw how the same negative energy that twisted my day into knots of anxiety and tension also came into play when I tried to meditate. Yes, I had blissful experiences that filled me with so much energy I couldn't sleep at night. But I rode on my longing for them like a witch on a broomstick, trying to storm the gates of heaven. Although my wish was sincere, the Perfectionist was there too, urging: *"**PUSH, PUSH, PUSH!**"* How could I (or anyone) push myself onto a higher level of Being?

Our determination to change deepens when we wake up to the fact that the Perfectionist always leaves us dissatisfied. Yet it took me a long time to realize I was never where I wanted to be or in touch with how I wanted to feel. How ridiculous it sounds when you spell it out. How could I possibly be where I'm not? But what an enormous amount of energy I spent trying! As I wrote in my journal: *How to be satisfied with who and what you are? How to stop spending your soul's energy questing after a dream? Wake up, Patty! Your future begins RIGHT NOW! Your new goal is not to get to some alternative universe. Your goal is to be right here where you are!*

At that moment I reconnected with my personal myth—the story of the high priestess and the Great Jade in the hidden valley beyond the mountains. Surely I'd identified myself with her unconsciously long ago, thinking I too could learn to look into the stone by moon or sunlight. That way I'd see all aspects of myself without flinching. But my longing had gone underground. Was she my ideal image, I wondered, or would Jung call her my Shadow?

As I delved deeper into my Perfectionist persona, more shocks followed. I discovered that behind my drive to be perfect lurked a secret satisfaction at the nobility of such a wish as well as a deep need to feel superior. What devious process led me from an urge for perfection to the need to be perceived as perfect? And why such seething anger against my own imperfection—and anyone else's for that matter?

The Tyrant gleefully hooked into this exploration, flaying me with self-hate after each new insight. But harsh as it was to acknowledge each flaw, it was also cleansing. That's what kept me going. And when I caught myself criticizing someone about something I'd probably done myself, I learned to swallow my condemnation and forgive my neighbor for being human, just like me.

Each moment of humility brought with it an enormous sense of relief. But it never lasted long. Soon a sneaky self-congratulation set in—how capable I was of subtleties of the spirit, able to recognize lying and deception in myself. "Peacock feathers!" snorted Gurdjieff's voice in my mind. My only escape from this rollercoaster ride of self-discovery and self-attack was to look deeper into the Great Jade stone.

When another fantasy surfaced—the secret desire to be one of the Masters—I cried out: *"How can I want to be what I'm not? What's going on here? Why were such figures hidden in my unconscious for so many years, only to shame me now?"* Further study showed me that the High Priestess and the Masters (Wise Woman/Wise Man) are two of the psychic energy fields Jung calls archetypes, powerful forces that can help guide or destroy us. Like many other archetypes, they live in us as numinous images— Mother, Father, Child, Adolescent, Hero, Lover, Warrior, and so on. But if we remain unconscious of their superhuman energy, it can seize us and drive us to extremes even though we're unaware how we are forced to act as we do.

As Edward Edinger explains in *Ego and Archetype*, if "an unconscious symbol is lived but not perceived…the ego, identified with the symbolic image, becomes its victim, condemned to live out concretely the meaning of the symbol rather than to understand it consciously. To the degree that the ego is identified with the archetypal psyche, the dynamism of the symbol will be seen and experienced only as an urge to lust or power."

It was hard to assimilate, but clarified much I didn't understand about my inner personas. These archetypes or energy patterns are part of our psychic structure—constellated in us at different moments of our lives. Jung compares them to the pantheon of Olympic gods, the powerful forces who kept the Greeks and Romans under their thumb. They had to serve them or suffer dire consequences. As he explains it, "Archetypes are like riverbeds, which dry up when the water deserts them, but which it can find again at any time. An archetype is like an old watercourse along which the water of life flowed for centuries, digging a deep channel for itself. The longer it has flowed in this channel the more likely it is that sooner or later the water will return to its old bed." (Vol 10, "Wotan")

If we can become conscious of how archetypes manifest in us, we'll be able to live in a more authentic way. And, once the hidden inner desire/tendency/dream is uncovered, whether you approve of it or not, best not to deny it or pretend it isn't there! Better to allow it into consciousness even if it hurts, and embrace the force that drives you. Listen to this mysterious presence, give it room to express itself and try to find a relationship with its energy. Marion Woodman advised us in a recent dream workshop: "When you're dealing with archetypal energy, keep one foot on the gas and one foot on the brake!"

Whether I'd been brought to this new place by the workings of a Tyrant or an Inner Guide, I was now divided against myself. Dogged by the image of an unending tug of war between two equally matched teams, I felt myself strung up in the tension of the taut rope between them as each tried to drag the other into the abyss. Jung calls this psychic situation "holding the tension between the opposites."

Happily, by then I'd recognized the wish for perfection was a form of inflation, with self-attack at the other end of the rope. When the Perfectionist sat on my inner throne, I'd become hypercritical and condemn anything that wasn't being done just right. No ordinary effort was ever good enough, so I must be super-perfect to be anyone at all.

Feelings of shame and guilt suffused me each time I caught sight of this attitude. I'd never be satisfactory! Once again I'd become the Tyrant's "worm in sheep's clothing." But when I dared to stand between these two terrorists and look down into the abyss between them, I faced my humanity, my smallness and the tremendous forces that moved me to action while, all the time, I'd thought I was in charge. Finally I worked up courage to ask the Perfectionist:

What's going on here?
WHAT DO YOU WANT TO KNOW?

Why am I such a prisoner of perfectionism?
YOU NEVER MEASURE UP TO STANDARDS. YOU NEVER DO ENOUGH OR DO IT RIGHT.

What human being could meet your otherworldly criteria? I'm human. Don't you accept that?
YOU WERE RAISED TO HIGH STANDARDS OF PERFORMANCE.

How about high standards of Being? I cannot be myself if I'm always concerned with performance. But who am I? Who is this "myself?"

BREATHE INTO YOUR BACK.

Startled by a suggestion so unrelated to the Perfectionist's usually arrogant attitude, I wondered whether someone in me could help as well as criticize. Perhaps I was no longer alone in this dark underworld of strange irruptions and desires my conscious mind knew nothing about. Could a friend be waiting somewhere in these murky depths?

AND YOU, WHAT DO YOU SEEK?

If, as I believe, we are all passionate about something, that must be true of you, too. What do you desire above all else? What makes your nervous system hum with excitement, gives you sleepless nights? I don't mean the ever-present anxiety that's almost like the air we breathe, but the beyond-ordinary goal that's hidden somewhere in your heart. It may be stored deep within your being, but it's there. Seek it out. It will tell you what you really want.

ALLOW YOUR QUESTION THE WEIGHT IT DESERVES

It's worth sitting quietly and focusing on this question for half an hour. Then write down what you really want on a piece of paper. Keep it with you at all times to remind yourself of what we continually forget in the busy byplay of our achieving lives: that our time on earth is conditional and limited. We need to give time to what spiritual teachers have called "the one thing necessary;" what we seek above all else.

TAKE A GOOD LOOK AT YOUR PAST
Tell your story as if you're writing to an intimate friend or sharing it with your children. To write down a summary of what you wanted out of life and where you've ended up, could be an eye-opener. What we write is often less colored by the subjective emotions of the moment. And if you really want to know where you've been, it may become clearer if you give it a third-person treatment. So commit to paper where you've been and who you think you are.

NEXT, WRITE ABOUT THE FUTURE
Where would you like to be five years, ten years, twenty years from now? What would that entail? If you want to travel, maybe it's time to learn a language and study the history of the places you'd like to visit. Whatever your goal may be, when you prepare for it in some practical way, it becomes more real. That helps you stay in the present, here and now.

WE NEVER TAKE TIME TO BE PRESENT
We hurry through our lives to get stuff done that has to be done, both for ourselves and for others. We meet our obligations and even take time out for a little fun and relaxation. But from time to time we recognize that we're stressed and stretched out on the surface of our lives—caught in a superficial busyness. It's a life without much depth, lacking contact with an innermost Self. Yet someone in us is thirsty for refreshment from the depths of our Being.

LOOK LONG INTO THE JADE STONE
As you look into the Great Jade, stay there long enough to see beyond the faults, disappointment or disapproval you may feel about your life. Focus on what you want, aside from every-day necessities. Then ask yourself, what price would you pay to get it? Because everything has a price. (But life already taught you that!)

IT'S A BALANCING ACT

We aspire to much that's beyond our grasp and drive ourselves onward to achieve it, just like the perfection I demanded of myself. Only when we give up unreasonable demands, and accept the uncertain human condition of life on earth can we meet our needs. That way, we come to what's real in ourselves and find our way to who we really are. Only God is perfect, and we don't live in Heaven!

SO FORGIVE YOURSELF FOR NOT BEING PERFECT

Admit to yourself that your dreams exceed your reach and that what you thought you wanted may not be your heart's desire. If that's the case, find the courage to give up what's superfluous. Even if you never figured out your heart's desire, it's there waiting for you. Maybe you never had time for it, but it haunts every act and every misstep. Look again into the Great Jade and see what's really going on under the surface pushme-pullme of your life.

LET OTHERS KNOW YOU ARE HUMAN

From pinpricks to major stabs in the heart, forgiveness heals. So next time you say something hurtful, interrupt yourself and apologize: "I didn't mean to say that, and anyway it was mean." Or "For years I've been jealous of your hourglass figure (or your beautiful dresses) because I can't seem to lose weight." Or even, "I've hated the fact that Mother always loved you more than the rest of us, but it's not fair to hold you responsible."

YOU MAY NEVER LOSE YOUR INNER PERSECUTOR

We may sense the shape of these archetypes, these tremendous energies that govern our actions and reactions. We may yearn to get rid of them but they aren't going to go away. However, we can begin to change how we respond to life. I rejoice that, in the long run, the need to see the truth about myself won the tug of war with the desire for perfection. But the Perfectionist never disappeared. On stormy days, that dried-up riverbed could quickly fill to the brim and drive me into anguished efforts to be 'right.'

MAKE A VOW TO RETURN TO YOURSELF

If you are like me, you'll find it's in your best interest to guard against that image of perfection, that tyrannical enemy of growth. Return to being "just me," even "little ol' me," as I sometimes call myself. At such moments of giving up the insistent Perfectionist, it often helped me to repeat the words of Thomas Merton in No Man is an Island: "It is...a very great thing to be little, which is to say: to be ourselves." What's more, that's where hope lies.

Eight: The High Cost of Loving

"Is it a sin, is it a crime,
Loving you, dear, like I do?
If it's a crime, then I'm guilty,
Guilty of loving you."
Lyrics by Gus Kahn / Harry Akst / Richard Whiting

To go or not to go to Peru? After college, I spent six years reporting for *Time*. Back in the office after an extended vacation, I yawned through the opening story conference, raced around town on interviews, and sat at my desk impatient for the week to end. At the ritual closing-night meal from 21 Club I avoided the usual bull-sessions and forgot to take a few extra desserts home for the weekend, along with a helping of veal birds. Without my understanding why, my frenetic life as a reporter had bumped up against a solid wall of resistance. Suddenly confused and uncertain, I also knew that at 27 I was too old to hope for marriage.

That's how the Great Adventure began. Invited to teach Gurdjieff's sacred dances to a new group of South Americans in Lima, Peru, I said yes to a two-week stint there. I could rev up my rusty Spanish and put off answering the questions that were beginning to burn in me about the meaning of my life.

I and the older companion assigned to lead the group were engulfed at the Lima airport by three big men. According to later report, the minute we appeared one of them declared: "This one's for me!" They pirated us off to our living quarters, a ramshackle house that teetered on the edge of a cliff, overlooking the sea. A whirlwind romance began with my new swain, which frustrated his parents because he broke off his engagement to one of the wealthiest girls in town.

After the two week interval, I returned to New York wondering whether an international marriage could possibly work. My Latin lover followed me the very next day, preceded by a huge bunch of white roses for my mother and red ones for me. That night he asked my stepfather formally for my hand.

Nine months later we had a New York wedding and a honeymoon week in the Bahamas, followed by a return to real life. We settled into a small house in Chaclacayo, a half hour's drive into the mountains. There the sun shone most of the year even when Lima was damp and cloudy. However, early every morning we left it behind and drove to the city so my husband could join his new law firm. He let me off at my sister-in-law's where I began the struggle to put together furnishings for our house.

Everything I tried to do met delay and frustration. First we must have a bed, which may sound simple, but none existed ready-made. To order and build one took more than a week. Added to that, tables, chairs, bookshelves, all made to order. The list seemed endless when I learned that, in Lima, only One Thing could get done per day.

Here's how it went: when my husband dropped me off, my sister-in-law was usually in the shower. We'd chat while she had breakfast. Late in the morning we'd drive off (at last) to accomplish our One Thing. Afterward, I'd lunch with my husband downtown, then read, take a stroll, go to a museum, etc. Gurdjieff meetings or movements classes filled most evenings, so it was often late in the night when we drove back up to Chaclacayo to look at the brilliant stars before going to bed.

My first Peruvian crisis unfolded when one of my children was vaccinated at birth with live tuberculosis. The BCG vaccine was a requirement for newborns because many Indians from the high mountains came to work in the capital. Lungs overdeveloped from oxygen-poor air in the Sierra, they easily caught and spread the disease.

Of course the vaccine wasn't supposed to be live. Years

later, I learned the Peruvian government had mistakenly dispensed live vaccine for three months. And while the pediatrician must have known it was TB, she never told me, nor did she mention that the medicine she prescribed must be taken for several years. So when the bottle was empty, I assumed that was enough. Six months later, another doctor insisted a new outbreak was just a superficial infection.

I became very frightened. Every food I gave the baby brought on diarrhea except for preemie milk and rice cereal. After a year of this, we flew to New York where a specialist confirmed intestinal tuberculosis. He prescribed the appropriate medicine, warned me to administer it for several years, and began to treat my anxiety as well.

A few months later, my husband was appointed governor of Loreto, the largest province in Peru (mostly jungle), with headquarters in Iquitos. We were to join him there. Fed by horror stories of the tropics, I prepared myself for parasites, spiders, snakes and a host of unknowns. But, first, I and two toddlers must be vaccinated against malaria and yellow fever.

We returned to Lima after six months in New York. The whole Peruvian family gathered to meet us at the airport at dawn, concerned for the future of the marriage. But true to the upside-down world of childrearing, all three of us had just fallen asleep an hour before landing. Tousled and gritty, we could barely focus. Next morning at dawn we flew over the Andes in a tiny plane. As we sucked oxygen through a tube, we stared, mesmerized, at the barren mountaintops that unreeled a few yards below us, as foreign to our eyes as mountains of the moon.

My state of high anxiety about the children, which had relaxed with civilized living in New York, returned with a vengeance. My first act was to get down on my knees with a bucket of water heavily laced with disinfectant, to rid our new jungle home of parasites. The wooden floor of the two bedrooms and living room seemed endless, probably because I scrubbed each area repeatedly, passionately engaged in killing off all our invisible enemies with no idea how much was enough.

Suddenly my husband's secretary was on her knees beside me, her sponge dipping in and out of my bucket. Maybe everyone else thought I was a crazy American (including my husband), but she, bless her heart, understood without a word what I was going through. She matched me patch by patch until we had finished the whole expanse of floor. Did that make me feel safe from the invisible enemy? Not at all!

The day became so hot my hands swelled, which forced me to take off my diamond engagement ring. I put it high on a shelf. The young Indian girl hired to help me disappeared the next day and the ring went with her. A few days later the police chief came to see us. He reported that she'd been captured and that a little torture might reveal where the ring had gone, but it was probably gone forever. "Forget it," I shuddered, unable to bear the idea.

After midnight that first night, I was wakened by scratching, scrabbling noises, which my husband assured me were coming from the floor above us, an unused part of the building. Yes, they were rats. I woke him up a second time a few minutes later, insisting I could hear them right under our bed. "You're right," he had the nerve to reply, "but I didn't want to scare you!" I rose up with a shriek as I visualized our small children in the next room under attack by a horde of rats. Next morning, rat poison was hidden in every crevasse.

Our home consisted of three rooms: two bedrooms and a wide living room with a view of the swift-flowing Amazon. The great river rushed below our front windows, endless and awesome, carrying small and medium-sized boats of every kind as well as rafts built of logs tied together and piled high with produce. In the rainy season, the Amazon rose twenty to thirty feet, while torrents poured from the sky so thick you couldn't see more than a foot or two ahead. We'd be drenched in seconds as well as shocked by the temperature drop, which could fall as much as 10 degrees Celsius in a few minutes.

Our kitchen and dining room were across an open patio, and beyond them, another patio connected to the government offices. At the center of our personal patio a small parrot twittered in a cage, a gift to my four-year-old daughter. She loved it, fed it and cleaned the cage every day. Well, luckily not every day. One morning, the handyman changed the newspaper and discovered a Loro Machaco under the paper—one of the deadliest snakes in the Amazon.

If you look at a map, you'll see that the province of Loreto occupies one-third of Peru. But at that time there were only 60 miles of roads and very few cars because most of the traffic moved in boats on the rivers. We often explored them in a small speedboat. We'd glide quietly down small tributaries of the Amazon, overhung with vegetation, and listen to the chatter of parrots, parakeets and monkeys as we scanned the banks for crocodiles among the half-sunken logs.

There were many official functions to attend, most of them evening events. The women would gather at one end of the room to gossip about children and clothes, while the men talked politics at the other. Then we'd all sit together at meals. It was pretty boring. More exciting were my duties as president of the Green Cross, an organization that provided medicines to the needy along the rivers. I gathered contributions from a monthly tea for a hundred women who supported the organization and, together, we ran a small dispensary on Friday afternoons. With the help of the Peace Corps, I arranged a month-long summer visit by a group of doctors and young people from Somerville, New Jersey. They treated the sick and helped build roads and schools.

One major daytime function was a ceremony at a remote village on the Putumayo River, near the border with Colombia, where few white people had ever been. The governor, the mayor, the head of Amazon University and their wives met at the airport, where the ladies hugged each other as usual. That's when they discovered my arms were slick with mosquito repellent and I became the butt of everyone's jokes.

We flew over a carpet of endless green treetops interrupted occasionally by curving brown rivers, until our amphibious plane splashed down onto the Putumayo. We skittered and jumped off the pontoons and onto dry land, then climbed past two lines of boy scouts standing at attention on both sides of a steep path. At the top of the hill a small canvas cover, stretched over folding chairs, protected us from the blazing sun in the village square.

Our seats were dictated by officialdom: dignitaries in front, ladies in the second row, assistants in the third. As the long speeches began, everyone but me wriggled and slapped at *la manta blanca* (the white cloak)—a cloud of insects so tiny you could barely see them. Suddenly someone leaned forward from the back row to ask if I had any more bug juice. "No one's laughing at me now!" I chuckled as my bottle was passed from hand to hand.

Three months after my third child was born, an army general brought his tanks to bear on the Presidential Palace in Lima one September night. He kidnapped the president and put him on a plane to Argentina in his pajamas. Next morning an army lieutenant visited me at dawn, while I breakfasted with the children, to warn me that the army was in command of the country and a detachment of soldiers would take over the governor's offices in an hour.

High drama! What did it mean? What to do? My husband in Lima, I was on my own with a baby and two small children. I hurried everyone out of the dining room to our private quarters, rushed to my husband's office, dumped all his papers into an empty carton and slid it under my bed. I figured I could always lie down and scream hysterically if the soldiers came in looking for it.

Confined to our three rooms, we waited all morning, wondering what would happen next. At one point, a rock crashed through our bathroom window with a note attached. It was from the head of the Amazon University. His car was right outside in case we needed to flee. We were to climb out the window and be driven to safety. Meanwhile, my excited children, who'd made many friends among the guards in our two years in Iquitos, wanted to go out and chat with the soldiers.

Every few hours I besieged the military governor in his office, demanding to talk to my husband on the phone. Unfailingly polite, he explained that this was a revolution. The telephone lines had been commandeered by the army while they took over the country. But by mid-afternoon he helped me get through. "Don't worry," said my husband, "I'm coming to get you on the first plane tomorrow morning."

His friends and family warned him that, as the deposed president's representative in Loreto, he'd be put in prison the minute he landed. But he counted on good relations with the local military over the past two years to keep him out of jail. And he was right. The next morning we watched the official black car, ours two days before, drive off to the airport to pick him up. What's more, aware of political unrest, my husband had shrewdly bought return tickets to Lima a few weeks earlier.

To add to the excitement, one of my stepfather's heart patients was executive vice president of Standard Oil, the company whose oilfield had triggered the military coup. I was summoned by a radio amateur to his jungle cabin to take a call from my parents, who said the executive plane was ready to fly in and pick us up. I replied that everything was fine—what else could I say with an armed guard standing beside me? We packed our things and fled back to Lima.

With no income and no place to live, we were in trouble. A friend lent us a low-rent house in the working class district of Chorillos, on the outskirts of the city. In another stroke of good fortune, I immediately found a job teaching first grade at the American School of Lima. My eldest child was now kindergarten age, so she and I went to school early every morning.

Christmas came soon with no money for presents. We

bought a tiny tree-in-a-pot, made a few decorations, gave each other little things. The warmth was there, the children were small; it was fun. From then on we always celebrated with a small living pine tree, and planted it in the garden wherever we lived. Decades later, our trees are scattered all over Lima, at least three of them now tall pines. One towers above the garden wall of a house in the suburb of Monterrico Norte, visible from the Pan American highway, on the right side as you drive south. Another rises tall and strong above a school in Monterrico. When the property was redesigned to build a school, the principal, who had helped us plant that tree years earlier, insisted it must stay. So it is now the centerpiece at the front entrance of Colegio Leonardo da Vinci, with all the school buildings designed around it.

For half a year, I taught first grade at the American School, then started my own pre-school. I patterned it after the United Nations' International Playgroup, which my daughter had attended for a few months in New York. The first IPG ever licensed outside the U.S. started up in my home with my own baby and small child plus five children. The next year we moved to Monterrico, out near the American School, and matriculated forty children. By the following year, we were well known, with ninety kids, aged two to six.

Along with the pre-school, I offered Saturday crafts classes for older children and a summer school. It was a wonderful experience for the whole family although we never made a profit. But as inflation spiraled out of control, I could no longer afford not to make money. And foreign countries began to send seasoned diplomats with older children to a troubled Peru.

Finally, after eight years, I had to close the school. In a day that seemed endless, I emptied the rented school building that had witnessed so much joy. Unable to utter a word, I vibrated with unexpressed rage, pain and tension as my husband and I packed toys into cartons and moved the brightly colored tables, chairs and bookcases I had painted eight years before, into a truck. They were to be stored in an empty room in the crumbling family mansion that was our most recent home.

Within days, I got a job teaching fifth grade at the American School. Although a fast learner, I'd never taught upper primary school. It was a struggle to stay a week ahead of the five subjects I taught to 25 fifth graders. At the end of the year I proposed a summer school unlike any they'd ever had, far beyond the familiar catch-up classes for the three 'r's. Four hundred students studied subjects from martial arts to stargazing to dance and painting, taught by 40 teachers and student teachers. It was an unqualified success and made the school lots of money, of which very little came my way.

That was the final year of my marriage. Less and less able to tolerate growing indigestion, I felt my body give way under my determination to keep the family together. Life with my husband had become replete with arguments, misunderstandings and inexpressible anguish. The realization grew that, although I cared so much for all my loved ones, pouring out my energy in an attempt to make everyone's life better, there was no one able to look out for me. My husband, like another needy child, absorbed all the attention I had time to give him. So, a few months after the summer school closed, I left Peru with my children, planning to spend a month with my parents in New York. I never suspected my body would refuse to let me go back.

WRITE YOUR OWN LOVE STORY

Innocence, rhapsody, joy, betrayal, bitterness, the dance of anger or of forgiveness. Tell it like it was. Write it down. We always learn more about ourselves when we commit to paper what we're thinking and feeling. That's something you've probably already discovered if you've been keeping up with these end-of-chapter suggestions in your notebook.

WHAT WAS YOUR DREAM?

Alternatively, you could explore the love story you wanted to be yours. In either case, if you can tell it in as much detail as possible, you'll learn something new. Guaranteed! But this may be the hardest exercise you're asked to do, to return in your mind and heart to a time of intense joy—or pain—or disappointment.

RETURN AGAIN TO YOUR CHILDHOOD

Who or what did you love most as a child? Was it a parent, a sibling, a real or imaginary companion? And think back not only to people. Perhaps your secret, dearest affection was for a doll, a bear, a bicycle, a baseball cap, a game you played, a place where you could hide away from the world, or something you loved most to do. Call any of them to the forefront of your mind and sit a few moments with the image, allowing it room and time to enter your heart as well as your mind.

GIVE YOURSELF THE CREDIT YOU DESERVE

We can be so busy with life's challenges we forget our own needs, especially when raising children or caring for someone who's ill. The urgencies of the moment, the deep wish to keep them safe, happy and well, can over-ride self-care. No matter how long ago you left that world behind, and whether or not you succeeded, it's important to honor how hard you tried to make life good for those you loved.

LET GO OF YOUR MISTAKES IN LOVE

If you feel you "made a mess of the best" (which my accused me of), forgive yourself for not knowing e‹ ‗… Remember, we're always beginners at life as it flows toward us. Recognize how little we know when we choose a mate, commit to a job or make our sometimes fumbling attempts to raise children. At every point in our lives, we're starting over. Since we learn as we go along, it's our mistakes that teach us, not our triumphs.

WHAT SOFTENS YOUR HEART RIGHT NOW?

Some of us are afraid of tears, but they can be very healing, so don't be afraid to allow feelings to well up in you as you try these exercises. Then ask yourself, what do you love right now? A dear partner? A summer day? A quiet place of rest? A challenging adventure? It's good to make a list, letting the words write themselves as you allow every suggestion or comment to come through without blocking any of them.

LOVING OPENS US TO GLORY AND DANGER

However, once you've been burned, it's hard to return to the fire. If that's your case, start out small as you attempt to understand what you really love. Scope out what attracts your feeling response: a person or a perfume or a thing. Little or big, it carries something of yourself. So put aside any judgmental attitude that what appeals to you doesn't really matter in the 'real world.' How do we know which is the real world, anyway!

WHAT WE LOVE NOURISHES US

Whatever moves me toward feeling is precious: it is the opening of myself to myself. Discover what opens you even when it seems trivial. For example, I love the feel of a silk shirt with long blousy sleeves that shush as I move around. Even more, if it's the color of burgundy wine. Why is that important? It makes me feel good. Everything that touches the heart feeds the soul.

FIND YOUR EQUIVALENT OF THE JADE STONE

Keep a concrete reminder of what you love with you. For example, on my desk is a rounded stone I picked up recently in the mountains as well as a special shell from a long-ago Peruvian beach. When I travel, I sometimes carry a tiny elephant with me to remind myself that I tend to forget the "elephant in the room." That's my code-word for emotions I refuse to experience when harsh things happen.

EXPERIMENT WITH NON-VERBAL EXPRESSION

Can you paint or sculpt or dance or play music in honor of something or someone you love? Just follow the paint as it leaves the brush or the piano keys as you wander on them, or the sound of your flute as you try to express an inexpressible feeling. Most helpful to me has always been working with clay. I love the feel of it as I squish it into shapes with my fingers. And the results often astonish me.

Nine: Lady in a Sandwich

"...a woman must steal attention if she's to remain sane...Each part of her is inadequately served, no matter how strenuously she neglects the other. In the end she doesn't solve the problem...She's carried along by time, as if riding in a stranger's car to an undeclared destination where the view is different, the altitude is different, and the old problem has been forgotten in contemplation of new ones...Women rarely achieve perfection of either life or work. As creatures of two elements, they are never sure which to leave and where to linger."
Joan Gould, *Spinning Straw Into Gold*

Within a week of our arrival in the city, I found a job as managing editor of *American Fabrics & Fashions*, a beautiful oversized quarterly magazine whose editor had died suddenly of a stroke. Hired to get the current issue to bed, I stayed on until the magazine closed down six years later. Following that, I organized a startup fashion magazine that aborted after three months. Then harsh times began. For six months I worked as a secretary for a temp agency, jumping from assignment to assignment every few days for $6 or $7 an hour. At last, on the advice of a friendly employer at *TV Guide*, I created my own agency, "Timely Temps." That way I could earn the whole $15 an hour he had been paying for me.

During this struggle I had no time to attend to an inner life, but it erupted anyway. Overwhelmed by guilt about the past and anxiety for the future, I was visited by a recurring fantasy: if I could cut my heart out with a knife, I wouldn't feel any more pain. Its sharpest stab came a year after our arrival in New York, with a friend's call from Lima: "Did you know another woman has moved in with your husband?" My instant thought: "That's to be expected!" but, blind to reason, I was convulsed by sobs.

And the pain didn't stop as I went about caring for children and parents, although I kept on telling myself, "I have no right to complain. I left him! People leave their husbands or wives all the time and they don't fall apart. What right have I to care so much?" However, since "rights" have little to do with suffering, I was depressed for many years. Psychotherapy would gradually waken me to this fact.

My job situation improved when I connected with former colleagues from Time Inc., the mammoth father-figure of a corporation where I'd worked as a reporter for *Time* many years before. Now, with three children in tow, I'd come full circle. Otto Fuerbringer, legendary managing editor of *Time*, who'd led startups for *Money* and *People*, was organizing another new venture: *Real Estate*. My stepfather rejoiced. "You're playing for the Yankees again," he said, his voice rich with approval.

Father Time absorbed my energy just as it had years before. Our tiny crew, Otto, two writers, two reporters and a photo editor, put out two successful issues, after which Otto invited me to be his second in command as associate editor for another start-up, *Leisure*. My heart leapt at the giant step up the ladder—a journalist's dream. Imagine the pleasure of writing about all those wonderful things you can do in your free time.

We put out four issues and were hard at work on a fifth when the downside of working for a Father Corporation reared its ugly head. The Magazine Development Division would shut down in December to get a once-only chance at a major tax write-off. Although there were four or five magazines under way, several of them already heading into the black, the tunnel-visioned MBAs in the corporate office salivated for that tax write-off.

I spent a bitter three months of job search from that haven of lost power and influence, until I landed a temporary assignment as communications consultant for the Rockefeller Foundation (another father-figure of a corporation). The following year, Time Inc. offered me a half-time job reporting a column on *Fortune*. By then my digestive distress had become so insistent that it was a relief to have a few days off each week to recover from pressure at the office while the children were in school. No energy remained, either mental or physical, for anything else. The tough challenge was how to get through each week.

It was during this time that I began to hear inner voices cry out at me during the day:

IF STOP BEING MYSELF I'LL BE MORE ACCEPTABLE.

I'M UNSATISFACTORY BECAUSE I'M THE WAY I AM.

MY ILLNESS IS EITHER MY FAULT OR I DESERVE IT.

DID I DO MY BEST? YES! IS MY BEST GOOD ENOUGH? NO!

A hysterectomy became necessary, followed a year later by violent chest pain that intimated a heart attack. It turned out to be an enraged gallbladder, which brought more surgery to remove it. Yet, through it all, I never quite fell apart. My heroic image of myself kept me going. I was one of the "walking wounded" as I managed to keep my job and care for my children.

That didn't change the compelling fact that self-care had become vital. I finally accepted that something was very wrong. A friend suggested I keep a journal, so I started noting my dreams and making commentaries on my inner ups and downs during the day. Perhaps writing in detail about my hurts, fears and frustrations would relieve the physical pain, allowing me a step or two back from my situation.

My early dreams spoke of the shipwreck of my marriage and the threat of forces beyond my control. Here are two of them:

Dream of Nightmare Forces: *a terrible shipwreck as one force slowly overtakes another, drowning it before our very eyes. We see one get weaker and the other stronger, as a father gets older and a son gradually gets power over him, in spite of all our efforts to save him.*

Dream by the sea: *Many people on the shore – and a tidal wave is coming. However the enemy is inland. We get a few things together to flee the oncoming water. But can we pass through enemy lines and not get caught? We have no choice as we watch the water rising faster through the grass around us, although we may be taken prisoner or killed. So we take a few things and flee inland. To what fate?*

I lived on the run all the time. My elderly parents, who for so many years had been a loving support, began to need care and hot dinners. My stepfather, a distinguished doctor, one-time president of the New York Heart Association, bid farewell to his patients (who continued to telephone anyway) and immersed himself in painting. My mother, a marvelous cook and homemaker who had served his complex needs day and night with joyful affirmation, began to decline. Soon her memory, his sight and their legs were all deteriorating at once as their exuberant independence gave way to dismay. The feeders now had to be fed, both literally and figuratively.

At the same time, my young adult children called on my attention in their efforts to find a solid place from which to build their own lives and become independent. When one or two of them were studying in different parts of the globe, long, expensive telephone calls and emergency funding were needed. At one moment, all four of us were on different continents. At other times, one of them nested in my apartment, in need of immediate support, fighting the discouragement of the job hunt. It was a constant struggle to keep going in face of the Enormous E's - eating and education.

I unburdened myself of some of these thoughts to a friend at lunch. When I paused for breath she smiled knowingly. "Ah yes," she said. "You are part of the sandwich generation!" I wondered what part I played. Certainly not the bread (although I earned it), so I had to be in the middle: the meat or peanut butter. A source of energy, calories and complex protein molecules, probably laced with salt, pepper and mayonnaise, or something oily to help me go down in a smooth and tasty way.

And who was dining on this three-generation meal that sat on the probably plastic plate of the late Eighties? My parents had danced the Charleston in the Twenties and survived the Great Depression on 75-cent helpings of scrambled eggs three times a day (straight for breakfast, with Ketchup for lunch, with onions for supper). Now my children were already international travelers who spoke two or three languages. And here we all were, trying to survive meaningfully in a world gone crazy.

Meaningfulness, for me, had to do with the development of greater consciousness. But what had most shaped my outer life was family. Both my family of origin and the one I shared with my husband and children represented almost everything I cared about. As an ideal, it drove me to keep going against all obstacles, gave meaning to my struggles and crowned my sense of usefulness. Yet my dedication to "keeping the family together" led me to illness, depression and a lot of suffering before I could separate from my husband and begin to understand my own personal needs.

This deep identification with family was surely due in part to the fact that my mother didn't have one. Raised by her mother's grandparents, who claimed they were her parents, she grew up feeling she didn't belong and wasn't wanted (see Chapter Two). She'd been a single mother with no financial assistance, whose courage kept us afloat throughout the Depression. Had I mimicked her situation—keeping my husband and three children going in an untenable financial situation?

In any case, this division of me into too many people trying to perform too many jobs was about to change. Shortly after the gall-bladder surgery, a voice cried out in a dream: *"ANY KIND OF HELP WILL DO!"* With that shout ringing in my ears, this lady-in-the-middle finally accepted the need for help. I began to look for guidance, starting at the Jung Foundation. An encounter with psychologist James Hillman revealed the dark side of my dedication to what he called "The Myth of Family."

Nothing in my over-crowded life could have kept me away from his day-long workshop, despite the fact that I was suffering from post-surgery cholestatic hepatitis. My daily treadmill went from constant pressure at the office to racing home in the evening to cook a "healthy" dinner for the kids, referee the battles between them, and attempt to get enough rest to stumble back to my job the next morning.

Hillman's opening words were shocking. In the first five minutes of his talk, he offered a series of grim statistics: one in four Americans lived alone versus one in seven twenty years before; two thirds of the children born that year lived in one-parent families, one in five with unwed mothers; and three percent of all adult males were in the correction system. How could we see the family as the norm, he asked, if the lives of 75% of Americans were a departure from it?

He conceded that the idea of family evokes warmth and comfort and that the child archetype in us longs for it. But, he exhorted us, "Break out of the ideal of family! You have created an imaginary story out of your past life with family, but it isn't what really happened. Marriage is a heavy-duty, dirty-diaper, realistic thing. Home is the most dangerous place to be, with the most homicides and the most hurt."

This was harsh stuff! I'd been totally "identified" with my own family, blaming its breakup on my own inability to handle my life. But this major figure in psychotherapy affirmed that family was largely a myth. Was it possible that my blind dedication to keeping the family together had been a bit crazy? Could I have been on the wrong track, compromising my health and my children's psychic wellbeing for a myth?

Continuing his attack on my Number One Identification, he added: "If the dress no longer fits, is it your fault? What is the guilt you are feeling doing for you?" Was he looking directly at me? I began to feel pressure in my sensitive gut. Was my guilt at breaking up the family the reason my relations with my teenaged children were so tense? It had certainly turned me into a too-permissive mother and an inadequate father-substitute! But he reassured me, and everyone there, that "You are never going to figure it all out or untangle it. You will just exchange one fiction for another."

That day performed a miracle on me, a powerful invitation to let go of my total absorption in my family. I rejoiced at the idea that I could put my consuming guilt away forever. At least it seemed possible in the heat of recognition, but it wasn't that simple. No magician's magic wand could erase my central focus of so many years. I sought out a Jungian psychologist and began an analysis. As I faced the turn of the decade in my fifties, hoping for a new beginning with help from a therapist, I turned to the newly arisen, cacophonous inner voices and began to dialogue with them.

)R A 180-DEGREE TURN?
in my life, pain and circumstances forced me to turn
at around, rather than continue to float downstream.
Although it was hard to move against the strong current of habit that opposed every effort at change, at least I was looking in a different direction. That's enough to start with and, in fact, a very big revision. If you decide to try it, don't be surprised that it's difficult. Take a few deep breaths and give yourself time to adjust to the new demand and the altered perspective as you struggle upstream.

A VERY SMALL BEGINNING IS A GOOD START
Find some small corner of your life that really disturbs you, where your desire for change is strong. Begin to examine it. Write down what you don't like about it. Then note down what you suspect was the cause of that particular situation. Finally, what was it useful for in your past life? Did it solve a problem you no longer have? Is there a way to approach it differently?

APOLOGIZE TO THE WORLD FOR YOUR FAULTS
It's time to give up the attack of guilt which surges up whenever you feel you haven't measured up. So every time you're shafted by a stab of guilt because you've done something wrong or not well enough in your own eyes, acknowledge it to the whole world. Look for the source of it—jealousy, annoyance, your own hurt feelings, whatever. It's an amazing fact that once we admit to our faults out in the open, we can let go of them and move on.

EXPERIMENTS ARE IN ORDER
Now make a few little changes. For example, if you're a pleaser, you could practice saying 'no' once a day. If you're a workaholic like me, it's a good idea to schedule a few brief interruptions into your program of daily activities. Promise yourself to respect them. Whatever your experiment, keep it small to begin with. A new life

isn't built in a day.

BE PREPARED FOR RESISTANCE
It's not easy to shift gears, even when you realize you've gone off course. Expect a strong wave of resistance, a mini-tsunami, a strong tail wind, or a subtle confusion. The new brain science tells us that whatever we've done repeatedly has carved out its own preferences in our activities: it's always more comfortable to go with the flow than create a new path. But we can build a new way of living through exercising in new ways.

REPETITION IS SLEEP-INDUCING; NOVELTY WAKES US UP
Recognize the power of habit over new beginnings and be sure to factor it in. That way, you'll be less overwhelmed by resistance and more able to undertake alternative ways of doing things—find new solutions to old problems. One of the exercises I tried, early on, was to take a different path to the subway every day for a week. It interfered with my habit of tuning out the world because my mind was forced to engage in checking out where I was.

DISCOVER HOW THE BRAIN WORKS
The latest brain research also proves why conscious intention is so important. It turns out that focusing our attention on something as we do it is central to creating new, better habits, rather than letting the mind drift wherever it wants to go. Nothing is as fixed in our brains as scientists used to think it was. New discoveries about neuroplasticity indicate that what we thought was rigid is, in fact, energy in movement. As Gurdjieff said, "You are where your attention is." Hold that thought!

EMPOWER YOURSELF
Find ways to give yourself permission to do things differently. Sometimes reward and punishment works but, other times, you need to call for help from a larger power. Either way, you will find extra energy to move ahead if you continue to remind yourself of

the importance of change, and the difficulty involved. I've found there's always help when I give up the conviction that I "know better." A sense of helplessness may be scary, but it may also be the most honest evaluation of the situation. And our wish for change may be more powerful than we think. There's a helper in each of us.

DIALOGUE WITH THE FORCES OF OPPOSITION
Try talking to the part of you that resists. Ask it what's going on. Why does it keep pushing you away from your intention? The best time for this is at the moment the resistance appears, but we don't always recognize what's going on then. So consider asking questions of the opposing forces next day, or whenever you come to realize that your conscious intentions have bumped against hidden barriers. Listen carefully. The answers you get may surprise you.

Ten: The Wounded Body

"The neglect of a deep, instinctual energy ultimately revenges itself in our somatic discords, compulsions, addictions or projections onto others."

James Hollis, *What Matters Most*

Pleasers like me live with a volcano in our depths. We swallow what we really feel, unconsciously convinced that if we don't comply with what's asked of us, Vesuvius will erupt and bury us all. As a result, my Nice-Guy complex, always dedicated to satisfy the (perceived) needs of others, had locked me into prison with an angry inner critic as my jailer. When his anger turned against me, I became physically ill.

As my marriage unraveled, my last few years in Peru were marked by gradually worsening attacks of indigestion. For a while they played a minor part in my busy life as I learned to stay away from heavily fried foods and hot spices. But over time they returned more often and sometimes verged on nausea. One day I threw up after eating. Did I ask myself what it could mean? No. I was too busy working at being a perfect wife, mother and teacher. So, for three days, I simply put my meals into a blender and soldiered on. It never occurred to me that more could be wrong than my digestive tract.

Happily, Tagamet had just come on the market to relieve gastric acid distress and I was one of its first Peruvian customers. Even so, the nausea returned from time to time. And the following summer, when I brought my family to New York to visit my parents, my gut announced there was no way I could go back. Even then I remained deaf to the message, convinced that after a good rest I'd get on a plane back to Lima. But each time my thoughts turned to going back, my stomach rose into my throat. Finally I heard my body's cry and knew that if I forced myself to go back, I'd probably die there.

But what had I done to deserve this, I who had always tried to do my best! I wrestled with this mystery as I began to study Jung's ideas. They introduced me to a larger world where powerful unconscious energies were at play. "A neurosis is an offended god," Jung writes, referring to the immense psychic forces that inundate our inner landscape and move us in ways we can't even imagine. In ancient Greece and Rome, he explains, these energies were called gods, but in the modern world, "The gods have become diseases." Without understanding that statement in the least, I was convinced it held some kind of answer for me.

As I struggled to free myself from pain and fear, Edward Edinger's comment in *Ego and Archetype* helped me develop a practice: "A symptom can be transformed into a symbol through awareness of its archetypal foundations...To be able to recognize the archetype, to see the symbolic image behind the symptom, immediately transforms the experience. It may be just as painful, but now it has meaning." My own experiments confirmed this. Whenever I sought images—the Tyrant, the barricaded crossroads, the huge snakes squeezing the life out of me—for times of acute suffering, my inner state would embrace a larger perspective.

Jungian analyst Joseph Cambray further clarified Jung's enigmatic statement at a conference I attended at *Jung on the Hudson*. "There's an archetype at the core of every complex," he explained. "Archetypes are the bones on which the flesh of our complexes is hung. They are universal—given from the start—yet can be called forth by what happens to us. Disease results when you don't respect aspects of your own being. It might help to ask yourself what's fixed and what flows?"

My task was to distinguish between the human, personal level of my individual life and the world of impersonal, archetypal forces and values. Archetypes have existed at all times and in all places. It's why Greek tragedy and other mythologies are so alive for us today. From primitive tribes to the flowering of civilization under the Greeks and Romans, such transpersonal forces were always recognized and treated as Gods. But today archetypal values are no longer recognized. Now that "God is dead," we humans assume that these powers are ours instead of forces to respect and reckon with.

This is like a man driving a car, filled with the sense of power that its strength and speed give him, which really belongs to the car! It corresponds to the psychological term *inflation*. That means that instead of worshiping at the altar of the Gods, we identify ourselves with these forces. When that happens we become infused with all kinds of obsessions and aggressive tendencies on the one hand, and fail to recognize the sources of our creativity on the other. Instead of a graceful sense of thankfulness as we honor these transpersonal forces, we become inflated and lose touch with our own reality.

Since these energies are God-given, they can turn into physical symptoms if I pretend I'm free of faults: i.e. that I have no aggression, lust, envy, etc. Psychologically speaking, the conscious person is out of touch with his or her libido, moving between states of emptiness and loss and those of inflation or aggression. In Jungian terms, the ego's relation to the Self is disconnected—the inflated ego thinks it is the Self. This unconscious lack of respect gives our shadow side power to hold sway over us and our actions without our being aware of it.

I reasoned with myself as I tried to take in this new angle on my situation. I believed in God, or higher forces, but who were my personal "gods?" And what were they telling me? As I focused on my daily moods and reactions, I discovered an undercurrent of anger. I wrote in my journal: *Me, angry? That's Number One Baad! Yet, although I can hardly bear to admit to it, I realize there's a very angry person in me whom I've never before allowed myself to see or feel. When my stepfather tells long rambling stories, I grind my teeth. After only a few minutes of conversation at a friend's house this afternoon, I was irritated and wanted to leave. At the store, I practically pushed someone out of my way to reach for the milk.*

After 50-odd years of refusing to acknowledge my anger, I woke up to an endless tug of war in myself. Anger was "bad" so I automatically condemned it. Yet here I was, enraged by the daily "oughts" that took up my time and angry at myself for feeling compelled to do them. Somehow I was caught between the need to fulfill unwanted duties and a rising inner demand to do something that was my own. I wondered, "What is compulsion?" The easy answer was: "I've got to. I can't not." But would the world fall apart if I didn't?

As my negativity surged out into the open, the physical pain increased. I wrote*: I'm imprisoned in tension and pain. I can't get out, even when I recognize what's going on. No escape. Only waiting and hoping the pain or anger goes away. But I'm not supposed to be angry! I'm supposed to be happy or productive or meaningfully engaged. What's more, this anger brings more reflux pain. Last night I could hardly sleep, waking every hour to drink milk and antacid. But it felt more like angry energy than pain. A dream image accompanied the words, "The view from Mount Rushmore." Those grim and frozen presidential faces must represent my frozen selves, carved in granite rock forever—huge, dominating, unsmiling, unmoving.*

"O.K." I said to myself. "So what kinds of anger do I feel?" As if I'd pressed a button, the answers popped into view: Anger at myself for not shaping up; anger at the world for not giving me my due; anger at life because my dreams haven't come true. "Ahah!" I said. "So here's a perfectionist, a victim, and a super-person who goes uncelebrated, cheated by herself, cheated by others, cheated by life. Where is this angry person hiding in me?"

It was impossible to reconcile this inner violence with my self-image as a calm, reasonable, thoughtful person, and no surprise that my digestion got worse at night. I'd often swig antacids after I groaned myself awake from dreams of criminals and cops, of being tortured along with a group of friends by bad guys. The dream themes told me there was No Way Out of some war zone surrounded by enemy troops.

Other dreams were set in prison. How was I imprisoned in attitudes and fears? In one dream, I was taken prisoner by enemy forces who wanted to take over the country and pressed me to betray "the others," people who lived in the same building, by signing false papers. What were my false papers? What power-driven part coerced me to betray my neighbors? Yet the theme of prisoner and enemy forces also registered on another level: all my life I'd been a prisoner of fear of disapproval.

In another vivid dream, I was in a large prison yard sporting a bright red cap. The whole scene, including my clothes, the other prisoners and the yard, was colored a misty, muddy grey-brown, except for that cap. Was this dream telling me I lived too much in my head, a prisoner of my turning thoughts? Were they what I always trusted?

You've probably noticed that dreams stir up a lot of questions but don't supply us with many answers. We have to bring our minds intentionally to stand at the gate between conscious and unconscious and hope their meaning comes by osmosis from one world to the other. As I began to accept and suffer the pain I'd refused to feel for so many years, new questions appeared. I was a Seeker of Truth, but how did self-discovery turn into self-attack? Was the sense of guilt that burdened me daily a refusal to see what was really going on? Above all, what could relieve the pain in my chest and belly?

Let me share one nightmare from which I woke breathless and frightened: *We're traveling on a ship and there's a murderer on board. One woman has already been murdered but most people on board know nothing about it. I hear a noise. I'm afraid but, since it might be a friend, I peek around the corner to look. It's very dark but I see a figure sitting halfway down some stairs. Frightened but determined to find out what's going on, I grab its feet to pull it down the remaining steps into the light. It comes thump, thump, thumping down, still in the sitting position. Another dead body! I'm terrified. Everyone on the ship is terrified. We can't see the enemy and don't know who it is, but an evil force is slowly murdering everyone on board. Who will be next? How can we stop it from happening?*

All next day, I was haunted by the image of that figure sitting on the dark stairs who came thumping down when I pulled at its legs. That evening, I tried a dialogue:

Why are you sitting in the dark?
BECAUSE I DON'T CARE.

What do you not care?
DARK, LIGHT, IT'S ALL THE SAME TO ME.

Why are you dead?
YOU KILLED ME.

What did I do wrong?
I DON'T KNOW.

Can I help you now?
PRAY FOR ME.

But I don't know who you are.
PRAY FOR YOURSELF THEN.

Deeply shaken, I asked, "What am I doing to myself?" Must I look more deeply into the smoldering anger that burned at the core of my Mrs. Nice-Guy personality, the anger that I refused to manifest? Anger wasn't an appropriate response to anything. And if it made me sick, best not be angry! But why did I avoid confrontation at any cost?

In the next weeks and months I began to experience many forms of anger: explosive, or quiet and mean. It crept through me like ground-fire until every part of me was set alight with rage. It built up from underground like lava ready to erupt from a volcano. Where did it come from? I was dazed and hurt, threatened by this powerful inner enemy who attacked me physically in the digestive system and mentally by forcing me to confront what I had so long denied—that I was angry at myself for not measuring up and at the world for not recognizing me.

As if I'd been hit by a body blow, I realized my deepest wounds came, not from the world, but from the anger I directed at myself. The Nazi torturer lived in me—some part of me had learned to torment me with relish. How could that be, when I was trying so hard to be right, to do right, to be the perfect mother, daughter, journalist? And the fact that I was doing a pretty good job at all three didn't help.

When the Nazi finally disappeared from my dreams, a savage Indian came after me, wanting to carve me up into body parts. One afternoon he even visited me in the daytime, as I walked to the park. My plan had been to leave early for an appointment and walk to it through Central Park but, when a glance out the window told me it might rain, I began to do other things. Finally, already in a hurry, I walked swiftly to a small nearby park for a quick turn. A savage anger erupted into dialogue:

IT WASN'T RAINING, SO WHY DIDN'T YOU GO OUT EARLIER TO CENTRAL PARK AS PLANNED?

I tried to reason with it, but the anger burned even harder, fueled by visualized pleasure of the long, unhurried walk I'd refused myself.

YOU FAILED YOURSELF. YOU "DID IT AGAIN."

Wild Indian, why are you so angry? I actually did get to a park, if not the big one.

YOU ARE UNBELIEVABLY STUPID AND CARELESS ABOUT IMPORTANT THINGS.
What particularly riles you?

YOU HAD THE TIME, YOU HAD THE AIM, AND YOU DIDN'T HONOR IT.
So it's when I don't keep my promise?

EXACTLY. YOU KEEP PROMISES TO OTHERS AND HOLD YOURSELF TO A HIGH STANDARD IN SOME THINGS, BUT IN THIS YOU JUST DON'T KNOW WHAT YOU'RE DOING.
What am I doing?

KILLING ME.
Who are you?

A PART OF YOURSELF.
How can we dialogue when you attack so savagely?

HOW CAN I DIALOGUE WHEN I'M NOT RESPECTED? YOU GIVE ME NO AUTHORITY HERE.
Why this give-no-quarter attitude even though I got to the park?

YOUR INTENTION WAS DIFFERENT. YOUR INTENTION WAS TO GIVE ROOM, TO TAKE TIME, AND YOU TURNED IT INTO A HIT-AND-RUN EXPERIENCE.
But many things have to be done more quickly or shortened. I can't always take "endless time." Why do you allow no leeway?

YOU'RE DISHONEST. THINGS ARE EITHER BLACK OR WHITE. NOW YOU'RE TRYING TO MAKE THEM GREY.
You're looking for perfection? Asking me to give all my attention to this side of things?

I'M LOOKING FOR YOU TO KEEP YOUR IMPORTANT COMMITMENTS AND NOT FUDGE AROUND.
How do I know what you consider important commitments?

YOU KNOW PERFECTLY WELL!
Do you know how much fear you evoke with your savage attacks?

NO, AND I DON'T CARE. RESPECT MY WISHES. GIVE ME WHAT YOU PROMISED.

I asked myself, "What am I missing here? What does this Savage need? What's his grievance? How could he or the Nazi be capable of resentment when they have no feelings?" But there was a big difference between them. The Nazi enjoyed torture but the savage was simply living the life he understood. While it involved murdering and scalping, it also included a love of nature, his true home. So it must have hurt him deeply to miss the walk in the park. To figure this out, I dialogued again with him:

Tell me more about the murderous rage you feel. Is it always there?
NO, NOT ALWAYS.

Why am I afraid of feelings?
BECAUSE THEY HURT!

Well, what was wrong with going to the other park?

I'VE HAD ENOUGH OF YOU AND YOUR ADAPTABLE WAYS. YOU'RE ALWAYS AVAILABLE.   WELL I'M NOT AVAILABLE, UNDERSTAND?

Is it worth asking you your arguments against going to the park?
WRONG QUESTION.

Are you so totally divorced from my need for nature, for inner quiet and spontaneous joy?
WRONG STATEMENT.

Then what should I be asking you?
WHAT DO YOU REALLY WANT?

As I took time to write down this and other exchanges, my digestive system began to calm down, at least for a while, instead of getting worse, as it had in early conversations with the Tyrant. Nevertheless, I failed to understand what my anger was about. It seemed so shameful. When I was called upon to solve a problem for a family member, a new bout of rage filled me. It wasn't triggered by what I was asked to do but by the disparaging comments and lack of appreciation for the time I'd spent doing it. I decided to dialogue with the anger itself. To my surprise, a new, authoritative voice spoke up:

Burning anger, what are you trying to tell me?
THAT I WON'T STAND FOR ANY MORE SHIT!

But isn't it just infantile irritation when one's own wishes aren't being met...wanting instant gratification, that kind of thing?
RESPECT MY VOICE.

Well, there's no problem about that. Of course I respect you, but how did you get into all this? I was dialoguing with the exaggerated childish rage that wells up in me.
HOW DO YOU KNOW WHAT IS CHILDISH AND WHAT IS OF THE CHILD? "A LITTLE CHILD SHALL LEAD THEM," AND "THE CHILD IS FATHER OF THE MAN."

True. But I feel helplessly in the grip...of so many things. Of anger, of frustration, of being servile—meeting peoples' needs, putting myself last. Then rage surges up from the depths as it does now, when I think of the scrawled 12-page thank-you letter I'm supposed to decipher, then type out, plus the many other letters I'll be given to type as well. I want to help but I can't do it all. I feel rage and helplessness at the same time.
I'M HERE TO HELP.

How?
TO POINT THE WAY. I WILL NOT ACCEPT ANY LONGER THAT YOU MAKE A DOORMAT OF YOURSELF. DON'T BE AFRAID, BUT LISTEN TO ME.

I've been afraid I'd be torn apart by this conflict. That you, unforgiving and outraged, would burn me up inside with gastric pain at the same time that my compulsion to accept what's asked of me would keep me functioning as before. Is there a way to end this conflict between the compulsion to be slavish and the anger it produces?
STICK WITH ME, BABY.

You are different. You're not a tyrant or stereotype like the others. I feel I know you. I trust you. Please help me.
THAT'S WHAT I'M HERE FOR.

OK. Then here's where I need help. I feel thwarted by the fact that I have no "free" time for myself. That's part of the anger: if I spend all my time "doing" for others, I feel robbed. I want to live in another kind of time, where no schedule or deadline awaits, which I call "endless time." But I know that's a dream. How can I find "endless time" in the middle of the reasonable but resented demands on my time, demands I've signed up for—authorized, so to speak?

ENDLESS TIME IS NOW. TAKE NOW, EVEN WHEN YOU ARE BUSY DOING THE THINGS YOU HAVE TO DO. IT'S YOURS. YOU ARE IN CHARGE OF YOUR OWN SCHEDULE. WHO SAYS YOU HAVE TO GO FROM ONE THING TO ANOTHER WITHOUT A PAUSE IN BETWEEN? LEAVE TIME.

Then are the demands I have to meet each day stumbling blocks or steppingstones?

YOU NEED TO LOVE THE CHILD IN YOU. IT CANNOT TAKE WHAT YOU CAN TAKE OR CARRY WHAT YOU CAN CARRY. THE MIND MUST CARE FOR THE BODY AS FOR A CHILD. EXERCISE IT, LOVE IT, LISTEN TO IT, DISCIPLINE IT, BUT NOT HARSHLY. AND NOT AS IF IT OUGHT TO KNOW BETTER AND TRIES TO MAKE TROUBLE ON PURPOSE, TO SPITE YOU. INSTEAD OF OVERKILL, OVER-DEMANDING OF YOURSELF, YOUR NEW MODE SHOULD BE OVERCARE.

LISTEN TO YOUR BODY
We all talk about doing this but, when we try, we discover it's not so easy. Our attention isn't available to take in its subtle messages. We're too busy thinking, planning, solving problems or ordering ourselves around. Which is O.K. After all, things have to get done. But at what price? And when we've had enough doing stuff, do we stash ourselves on the sofa in front of the TV in a state of collapse? (The body isn't too happy with that either!)

YOUR SYMPTOMS MAY TELL YOU WHAT'S WRONG
My gut revolted when I couldn't digest my life. We often say, "I can't stomach it," or "my gorge rises." Studies of neurosis show that paralyzed people who confront their inner demons have been able to walk again and speechless people have found their voice. "Symptoms are expressions of a desire for healing," says James Hollis: "Rather than repress them or eliminate them, one must understand the wound they represent." (*Swamplands of the Soul*)

LEARN TO READ
When someone frowns or smiles, backs away or comes too close, that's body language. There's information in almost every part of the body when you learn to translate it: a mouth can be grim with annoyance, lax with alcohol or firm with purpose. Tightly crossed legs can say "I won't let you in." Arms that grasp around the torso often do so to defend the heart. We can smile with or without our eyes, open our arms wide to greet someone or move away when they enter the room. That tells anyone who notices these things whether we/they are welcome.

IT'S A NEW LANGUAGE
Truly, the body speaks a different language from our customary left-brain way of seeing life. The real challenge is to learn that language. It's even possible, at times, to understand my body's needs without the intervention of the head. Or, rather, if I can I hear the complaint and intuit the need, I can bring my mind to help

solve the problem. Otherwise, my know-it-all head makes assumptions about my body that may not be at all accurate.

NOTICE THE RUNNING MONOLOGUE IN YOUR HEAD
Much of the time a meandering flow of associative thoughts runs on in our heads. Notice how one thought leads to another in accidental connections that often have no real relevance. It could go on forever, and leads nowhere. However, it distracts us from the reality we are living at each moment. Because we live mostly in our thoughts, the blood, flesh and bones of us is often unknown territory. But it's central to understanding ourselves better and freeing ourselves from the Tyrant. According to Marion Woodman, "The body is the unconscious in its most immediate and continuous form." (Addiction to Perfection)

SHOULDERS ARE A KEY TO RELEASING TENSION
If you take time to experiment, you'll see how identification with busy thoughts centers your energy in head and shoulders and can lead to sore, tight muscles as you carry your life like a burden. If you raise the shoulders as high as possible, then let them drop of their own weight, you can release some pressure and tension. There's physical and mental relief if you can let your shoulders go, even momentarily, as if shrugging away your problems.

OVERFOCUSED CONCENTRATION CAN ALSO TAKE US AWAY
When we've been concentrated on some assignment to the point of getting a headache, experience tells us we can bring ourselves back to earth by going for a walk or engaging in physical movement. Yet we seldom realize how important it is to shift our thoughts into body awareness as we go about our chores. That allows us to stay on the ground, even while we work, rather than fly up in anxieties, dreams or imagination.

ANCHOR YOURSELF

Our ego is afraid of change just as it's afraid of death, which is why it wants to keep things exactly the way they are. Yet as we forge a new connection between our sense of self and the conscious life we lead, it can expand its somewhat narrow view of things to embrace a larger, more mysterious world. The body is an anchor for that effort. Imagine you can grow roots consciously from your feet down into the earth. Stand like a tree. Begin to notice sensations you never attended to before.

HOW DO YOU CARE FOR YOUR BODY?

Gurdjieff likened our automatic thinking machine, which Buddhists call the Monkey Mind, to an old-fashioned London cabby who wants, more than anything, to sit comfortably in a pub and have a beer. He compared our emotional life to a horse and our body to the carriage it pulls. A driver who spends most of his time in a bar, spending the horse's feed money on his drinks and giving little thought to oiling and caring for the carriage, isn't doing his job.

WHAT ARE ITS LIMITATIONS?

The body tends to pay me back for inattention. It drags me down in fatigue. Or, if I'm riding an adrenalin rush to get stuff done, it will pump me up to go until I collapse, drained of energy. Yet when I accuse myself of being lazy, as I often do, I haven't been listening. The body truly wants to be active, but not if I treat it like a slave or a donkey I beat whenever it isn't following left-brain orders.

DO ONE THING AT A TIME

Your thoughts can travel to a thousand places in seconds, but your body can only do one thing at a time. You may think that's a curse, but believe it or not, it's a blessing. Mindfulness is about filling the body with mind. As you give up wandering thoughts and become attentive to every action, you become rooted in the present moment. That's where you can live deeply, rather than superficially. That's what it means to be embodied.

Eleven: "The Shadow Knows..."

"One does not become enlightened by imagining figures of light but by making the darkness conscious."

C. G. Jung, (*CW 13*)

Do you remember the radio program called The Shadow? When our parents were out, my brother and I tuned into this story about a crime-fighter who had the power to "alter men's minds so that they cannot see him." We shivered deliciously as a sepulchral voice asked: "Who knows what evil lurks in the hearts of men? The Shadow knows..." Fade in that horrid, eerie, meaningful laughter—as alive in my ears today as when I was nine years old.

When I began to study Jung's ideas, I was reminded of my attraction to that forbidden program. He spoke about the shadow side of each human being. It was hard to believe how much of me could be hidden from my consciousness. In fact, it was a threatening thought!

According to Jung, our shadow side develops very early, from a sorting process that continues all through childhood and youth, as our ego decides what's appropriate for our picture of ourselves and our identity-in-the-world. Aspects our parents disapproved of or urges that made us uncomfortable may have been stored deep in an inner vault, far from awareness.

The shocking truth is that how we think of ourselves today isn't all of who we are. Our self-image is largely based on what our society and our immediate family valued or criticized. And we either accepted it—trying to fit in, to "belong," to avoid conflicts with "the norm" the world presented to us—or rebelled against it. Much of what's real in us, devalued by our conscious sense of self, has been stored in an unconscious world within. But no matter how much we X'ed these aspects out of our awareness, they're never lost, just hidden deep in a Shadowland. Unknown to us, they live an emotional, possessive, autonomous life of their own.

"This shadow side has got to be bad," I reasoned. After all, it was full of subjective personal judgments, animal urges, antisocial reactions, pet hates and refused temptations. I desperately wanted to clump all that dark stuff together and get rid of it. Yet Jungians insist that valuable parts of us are also deposited there, along with long-ago infantile demands, "shameful" thoughts and violent emotional reactions.   An excellent source of writings about our shadow side is *Meeting the Shadow: The Hidden Power of the Dark Side of Human Nature,* edited by Connie Zweig and Jeremiah Abrams.

The work of healing begins with rediscovering and reintegrating what was hidden in that vault. As James Hollis wrote in *Why Good People do Bad Things*: "Working with the Shadow…is working toward the possibility of greater wholeness. We will never experience healing until we can come to love our unlovable places, for they, too, ask love of us." Why? Because our shadow side harbors a great deal of energy, undeveloped talents and unexpressed human potential that can serve us if we dare to explore it.

But unless and until we accept that a scary part of ourselves exists, we remain convinced we're the person our ego has chosen to be, along with the personal set of prejudices we absorbed from family and society. And the more I deny the shadow's existence, the more power it has to subvert my conscious intentions.

Once I decided to investigate the possibility of a Dark Side, there were plenty of clues to help me scope it out. Any strong emotional judgments and reactions with which I defended or reassured myself became suspect. For instance, an inner warning bell might buzz whenever I did something I didn't really mean to do, or felt irrational irritation at the attitude of others, or heard an undertone of vehemence in my insistence that "I'm not like that!"

or "That's not me!"

Each time I discovered an aspect of myself that couldn't tolerate my Nice-Guy efforts to please people, I tried to listen. But since I'd always thought pleasing others was a virtue, it was difficult to accept that it had a dark side. However, once I admitted to it, an inner door opened to a new view of myself. I began to wonder whether some of my other assumptions might be wrong as well.

However, nobody forces us to step into Shadowland. There are ways to escape the reality of our dark side by projecting what we don't like in ourselves onto others, which allows us to think they or the world are to blame for our discomforts and failures. But projections isolate us. They create unreal relationships and blind us to the reality of our shadow aspects. So I finally determined it was better to explore them than bury my devils deeper.

My dialogues became a "royal road" into a shadow world full of complexes—fragmentary personas that have an autonomous existence in the personality. It made sense to think of each complex as an enclosed energy system with the power to produce emotional reactions and provoke irrational responses. For example, any time I reacted with unnecessary vehemence or felt shamed by what someone said, a complex had almost certainly been touched.

The good news is that when we consciously admit to our complexes, they lose some of their power. Not that they'll ever disappear. We'll continue to be confronted by what we've devalued and discarded until we can embrace it as our own truth. It's not easy to find a path through all that's strange, unknown and unacceptable to the conscious mind in Shadowland.

The study of dreams leads deep into the shadow world. Jung called dream figures of the same sex as the dreamer shadow figures. They are more easily recognized than our deeper projections because they live in a layer he called the Personal Unconscious. The first shadow figure I met in dreams was the Blonde Bombshell...a loose woman with a cigarette between her over-rouged lips and a provocative sway of the hips. She represented all I consciously despised in my own sex as slut-like. At the same time I had to admit I was fascinated by such freedom from strict (and safe) morality. But how annoying if this was my shadow self! And how could knowing about it help me? Was I supposed to tear off my clothes and dance naked on a cafe table to find my true self?

Another major shadow figure visited me in the plain light of day. I dubbed her Mrs. Rigid, a persona who liked to have things one way and no other. She first joined me on a visit to my birth father at his beautiful home-on-the-Gulf in Florida, where I planned to recuperate from some highly stressed, 12-hour days at *Fortune*. But my psyche had other ideas.

I arrived late in the afternoon and immediately took off my shoes to walk on the beach. At last a chance to unwind! I would stroll barefoot in the warm sand, listen to the sough of the sea and perhaps even catch a beautiful sunset. But Mrs. Rigid got there first. She was on top of my every move, insisting I glance at my watch every few minutes to calculate how long I'd walked in one direction, how late it was, and when it would be time to start back.

This organizing demon was on my case all week, incessantly preoccupied with what time it was and what activities were "good" for me. She seldom let up her stern intention that I was to use my time well, insisting on when I should take walks, when go swimming, when write or sit in the sun—even when it was time for a cup of tea!

You'd think I could argue myself out of this creature of intense habit but try as I might, I couldn't make comfortable, relaxed choices based on my state of the moment. Even more disturbing, I half recognized myself in Mrs. Rigid's limited, narrow-minded approach. But I wasn't ready to go there yet. Some part of me refused to entertain such a thought because I didn't like where it led. No way would I dialogue with her!

A year later she reappeared at my father's beach house again. (She must have lived with me all the time but I never noticed her.) Once more I felt locked into a suit of armor as Mrs. R. programmed each detail so I could occupy every moment with sterling usefulness. This time it really upset me. Hey! I was on vacation! Why was she there, and why was she so darned RIGID? Hmm. Was there a panicked person in me who needed to learn to shift plans in midstream? If Mrs R. wasn't there to tell me what to do, who would make decisions for me, caught as I was in a jungle of *oughts* and *shoulds*?

These questions burned in me the next morning as I walked along the beach. Suddenly my inner state shifted. It was as if I were walking hand in hand with Mrs. Rigid on one side and a young child on the other. Some unknown energy passed through me from one to the other, connecting them. For a moment, I was free of the demands of both.

That was when I first realized that I could serve as a bridge between different parts of myself—in this case, the disapproving adult and the frightened child personality fragments. They seemed to be perpetually at odds, but as soon as I attended to both of them at the same time, an exchange seemed possible between them. A prayer infused my heart at this epiphany: to remember that communication between my child and my critic could only happen if I managed to be present to both of them at once.

Jung called this simultaneous awareness of conflicting sides of oneself, "a movement out of the suspension between two opposites, a living birth that leads to a new level of being, a new situation." *(MDR)* Although it can be a painful experience, a new level of consciousness emerges as we integrate the tension between two opposite parts of ourselves.

Marion Woodman referred to this difficult-to-bear psychic experience as "life's greatest challenge." She taught me that when we don't live in our bodies, rooted in our nature, we live like shadows. As she wrote in *The Ravaged Bridegroom*: "A disembodied woman is vulnerable to invasion by Medusa. If, on the other hand, she commits herself to embodiment, she will experience the agony of the thaw as her molecules awaken to the pain of past and present...As she becomes acquainted with the outcast Magdalene buried in her own tissues (my Blonde Bombshell?), her perfectionist Madonna comes off her pedestal and, stones or no stones, forgives herself and the rejected beauty within. In their embrace, they become one radiant human woman, no better, no worse, than she was born to be. 'Home' becomes her body which accepts suffering as a necessary part of her soul's yearning to know herself."

How well she described the pain that inhabited me every day! And what a relief to know I wasn't just a crazy woman who had weird dreams and talked to herself on a computer! With Marion's encouragement, I dialogued more frequently and far more attentively with whatever aspects of myself thrust themselves forward.

When I finally found the courage to dialogue with Mrs. Rigid, I was forced to recognize my habit of inner hurry. As I wrote in my journal: *I see, out of the corner of my eye, a person I used to think was me, someone always busy, who rides on my energy without ever slowing down. Business as usual, she seems to say. She glides along the surface of my life, reacting to what's happening, making suggestions, making changes, doing stuff. But it's not me! Behind her is someone she refuses to listen to and never permits to catch up with her.*

Who are you, busy, busy person, and why can't I just be quietly myself?
YOU CAN BE ANYONE YOU WANT, DEARIE. JUST DON'T GET IN MY WAY!

Wait a minute, please. How do I get in your way?

YOU'RE ALWAYS HUNTING, QUESTIONING, INTERFERING, MAKING MOUNTAINS OUT OF MOLEHILLS.

But I thought that busyness, the ferreting out what's going on, was coming from you!
NO INDEED. YOU'RE THE FERRET. YOU'RE THE HUNTER, THE SEEKER, THE QUESTIONER. I JUST GET ON WITH MY LIFE.

But what kind of a life is it? After all, we live together...
DO WE? WELL, I'M JUST GOING TO IGNORE YOU AND YOU CAN DO WHATEVER YOU WANT.

How can you ignore me if we share the same skin?
MOVING ON, MOVING ON, NO TIME FOR ALL YOUR WONDERING, WANDERING, THINKING STUFF OVER.

But if you're getting on with your life, where are you going?
(NO ANSWER)

Why is it sometimes amazingly hard to see what's right in front of you? It took a long time to realize that Mrs. Rigid wasn't strict because she knew better, but through fear and loneliness. She planned things carefully so life would remain safely familiar. Like the Frightened Child, Mrs. R. needed help and affection and only felt a sense of security when every free moment was organized ahead of time. This discovery was confirmed by the fact that, once my plans were in place for the day, I felt a subtle sense of relief. I wouldn't be alone with nothing to do and no way to fill the next hours. So after I got to know her better, I asked Mrs. R. for guidance:

I turn in a vicious circle between the clarity and warmth of an inner relationship with myself, and the prison you keep me in. When will I be less fragmented?

WHAT IS YOUR PRISON MADE OF?

I don't exactly know. My fixed beliefs; my fears. Sometimes I feel physically tied down, as if snakes were writhing around my body, squeezing tighter and tighter. I used to think I was supposed to accept life, whatever happened. But must I accept this prison? If so, why do I feel such an anguished need to live in a larger world of warmth and freedom, where I can breathe?

THERE IS NO FREEDOM IF THERE IS NO FREEDOM FROM RIGHT AND WRONG.

Bingo! Being right, or avoiding being in the wrong, was always high on my list. But I'd never realized how deeply it mattered to me. Was Mrs. Rigid saying it was no longer useful? Yet how could I accept my human failings and let go of the deeply ingrained need to be right? How to give up the strident demands of my organizing mind which, like Mrs. Rigid, determined in advance how everything ought to unfold?

Mrs. R. made her opinions into a religion. She was a mind-driven, disconnected piece of me that made it difficult for me to respond to the needs of each moment. Once I absorbed this fact, I discovered her cousin, The Editor. Always sure of herself, this persona held sway in my business meetings, quickly passing judgment on other people's suggestions, disposing of them, denying them, affirming the "right" views. The Editor was full of opinions and self-assurance, as if she knew everything. Newly suspicious of the "incisive mind" I'd always been proud of, I kept an eye open for her and discovered that she also edited me when I was alone.

You might well question how important is all this hunting down of shadow stuff. Is it just another form of self-involvement?

Does it serve any useful purpose? Jung was convinced that it could help change the world. Anyone courageous enough to recognize that the other guy isn't necessarily at fault, anyone who has discovered how we tend to project our own shadow onto others and works to absorb it back into him or herself, lightens the world's burden of confusion and negativity. "Such a person knows that whatever is wrong in the world is in himself, and if he only learns to deal with his own shadow, then he has done something real for the world. He has succeeded in removing an infinitesimal part of the unsolved gigantic problems of our day." (*CW 11*)

As we gradually integrate our shadow parts, we begin to own who we really are. But the search for authenticity never ends, as I discovered much later at a Haden Institute Summer Dream Conference. One of the speakers referred to "The Unlived Life," a course of action we may have unconsciously longed for, but never allowed ourselves to pursue.

Appalled at the new depths that opened under me, I asked myself, "What's my unlived life? How can I discover it? If my decisions are based on pain and choices I've made to avoid pain; if I don't like change and am desperate to keep things the way they are (under the control of Mrs. Rigid), who or what can help me?"

That same evening, I pondered these questions at a silent workshop where a small group of us made figures out of clay. Suddenly my hands began to move swiftly of themselves. An hour of pressing and twisting the clay produced a dwarfish figure. I stared at this creature—mostly huge head and great, unhappy eyes—and it stared back at me. My eyes flooded with tears as I ran to my room clutching this little figure, threw myself on the bed and went into a deep sleep.

All week long I asked myself, "What needy, unhappy person does this gnome-like figure represent?" Finally I found the courage to ask what it needed from me. The answer was immediate: *HELP.*

What kind of help can I give?
I AM A PART OF YOU.

I understand that, but what to do?
SEE ME. RECOGNIZE ME. CARRY ME WITH YOU
WHEREVER YOU GO.

Why do you have no torso?
I'M NOT PERFECT!

What has been denied you?
LOOK AT ME AND YOU'LL SEE.

You are mostly head and mostly an anguished cry for help. I
suspect you are my despised part. Yet I see you not as a shadow
figure but as the substance of my inner nature. Not someone or
something else, but me!

Was I supposed to help this inner dwarf, or was it there to
help me? I took it home, put it on a prominent shelf where I
continue to look at it and try to decipher its mysterious message. As
Donald Kalsched said, "When the banished parts of us return and
we can hold them with compassion, a sense of the divine often
enters our lives as a sense of wholeness." Was my little gnome a
messenger from the divine to help me become more whole?

WELCOME TO A WALK ON THE DARK SIDE!

It's not easy to find a path but if you're game for it, dreams and reveries can be very helpful. Look carefully at the male or female apparitions that visit you. Jungians identify dream people of the same sex as the dreamer as Shadow figures, but anything that's strange, unknown or seemingly unacceptable lives in Shadowland.

A RIVER RUNS THROUGH US

Deep under the dynamics of our daily life flows a hidden river of unconscious activity. It tries to compensate for our fixed conscious attitudes and our domineering complexes by often-alien shadow messages. Through dreams, associations and unconscious reactions, our soul's energy seeks to communicate with us. It invites us to open to a larger understanding.

ASKING QUESTIONS CAN HELP

Shadow aspects have a strong emotional quality. Here are some questions you could ask as you try to understand your own Shadow figures: What are they trying to tell you? What ticks you off about them or irritates you in your daily life? Which emotional reactions are out of proportion? When does a friend's gibe induce a volcanic response? Whose traits make you uncomfortable? Who in your life is unbearable? All of this may well be related to something hidden behind the screen of your ego.

WHAT DO OTHERS THINK OF YOU?

And how much does their opinion matter to you? It's important to focus on your public picture of yourself and the price you pay for keeping it up. Is your life a continuing performance, as mine was? I was doing my darnedest to be the perfect wife, the perfect mother, the perfect daughter and the best of all journalists, as well as the helper of anyone in trouble. Even as I write that down it sounds exhausting!

A TENSE BODY AND OVERBLOWN EMOTIONAL REACTIONS ARE KEY SIGNS
What are your convictions about yourself? Do you become tense
when others fail to accept your picture of yourself ("I get no
respect!")? Write down your answers to all these questions and
begin to make a list of when and why you get annoyed at others.
You can mine the visceral reactions that surprise you or that you
project onto other people. Whatever makes you uncomfortable or
produces anxiety can lead you to your Shadow.

EMOTIONS HAPPEN TO US
We usually think we are expressing ourselves when we feel emotions
but, according to Jung, emotions "are not an activity of the
individual but something that happens to him" (Aion, CW 9). This
helpful discovery takes the onus off some of our Shadow activities.
We often can't help ourselves since unbridled emotions usually
appear "where adaptation is weakest."

SEEING THE TRUTH CAN SET US FREE
Although we can't control our emotional reactions before the fact
and will probably act in the old way again and again, we gradually
become more aware of what's really going on. In the beginning it
may be hindsight, but even if recognition comes later, a powerful
energy is unleashed as soon as we face the truth. It cannot be
overvalued. Seeing what's really happening is the key to change.

"HOLD THE TENSION OF THE OPPOSITES"
Jung recommends that we become aware of both sides of ourselves
at once—for example, the humble and the arrogant—and accept
that they both exist in us. When we act without choosing too fast
or reacting too quickly, when we allow time to take in both sides of
any situation, we can scope out our hidden shadow side. To live our
dividedness is a painful but transformative experience.

THE PAUSE THAT PERMITS CHOICE
These days, when my mind insists but my body or feelings object,
I've learned to stop for a moment. Quite simply, to pause. That

allows me time to make a choice or renew an intention. Only after I've reviewed a situation can I consciously select what to do next and act on it. I may well decide to continue concentrating on what I'm doing, but only after a drink of water, a call to a friend or a walk to the store. Or perhaps I'll discover my stomach is upset or my body aches, pains that may be a direct result of my head's greediness for all my attention.

WHAT TO DO SO YOU CAN MOVE ON?
First commit to a conscious choice between letting old psychic habits continue to dog you and the hard work of making changes. Why is it so hard? Because so much of what long ago set your habits in place lives below your awareness. The old ways are comfortable and change isn't. But as you begin to realize what you lose by not making the effort, it becomes easier. As T. S. Eliot said in The Four Quartets: "The way in is the way out." To make changes, we must first delve deeply into what's going on right now.

OUR SHADOW LEADS US FORWARD
We dig up the past in order to uncover what hinders us today. Jung asked himself, "What is the necessary task which the patient will not accomplish?" (CW 4) And, as James Hollis pointed out in Swamplands of the Soul, "invariably, the task involves some new level of responsibility, some more honest encounter with the shadow, some deepening of the journey into places we'd rather not go."

HONOR YOUR SHADOW
As Robert Johnson advised us: "Our shadow costs nothing and is immediately—and embarrassingly—ever present. To honor and accept one's own shadow is a profound spiritual discipline. It is whole-making and thus holy and the most important experience of a lifetime." (Owning Your Own Shadow)

Twelve: The Tyrant Speaks

"A nervous tyrant lives in each of us (who) may rise up at any provocation to stifle dissent, or crush the alternative that wishes to come into life through us."
James Hollis, *What Matters Most*

Although the Tyrant was my major dream figure, he was far above noticing someone as unimportant and powerless as I. Yet there was no escape from him—his spies were everywhere. He ruled my whole "country" through secret agents, murderers and armies on endless maneuvers. His minions were dispatched to keep me and my Hero-self under his thumb. And during the day, his alter-ego—my Inner Judge—proclaimed how stupid or forgetful I'd been. He was always on my case, harshly critical of just about everything I did.

Why this constant attack? And was there any way to escape the physical pain and emotional anguish it produced? In urgent need of figuring out what was going on, I began Jung's Active Imagination experiment by calling on my Tyrant. My first exchange with him (see Chapter Five) frightened me, but my bones told me this was a path I must follow. So, burdened by pain and with little hope, I sat down at my computer a few days later to ask:

Who are you and why do you attack me so?
YOU ARE A FOOL!

I didn't ask who I was, but who are you?
THE GUIDE OF A FOOL!

Do you think attack or invective helps in guiding someone?
I HAVE TO MAKE YOU LISTEN TO ME.

Why won't I listen?
YOU NEVER DO.

What are the things you value?
DOING SOMETHING WELL, BEING AWARE, EVERYTHING IN APPLE PIE ORDER, FRIEND OF ALL THE WORLD. GOOD GIRL!

Why is there so much pain in our relationship?
BECAUSE YOU WON'T LISTEN.

I'm going to try to listen to you more, but at the same time, I may not follow your advice.
WHAT ELSE IS NEW?

While my exchanges with the tyrant were unpleasant, I hung on, determined to find some clue to what was happening in me. A few days later, I asked:

Why are you always after me, even in the most secret ways? When you say, "Why don't you just grow up?" it sounds like you mean I should give up hope, accept cynically that life is misery. Why?
YOU DEFINITELY NEED TO GROW UP, GET WITH IT, ACCEPT WHAT'S REAL INSTEAD OF LIVING IN A DREAM.

I agree with that, but why is the tone of your voice so cutting, stabbing, hurting me on purpose?
WELL, THE CHILD HAS GOT TO SEE HOW THINGS REALLY ARE.

But the child doesn't need to be punished with threats. Especially when it's possible we don't know how things really are. Yet you keep suggesting you do know and that life's the pits.
WELL IT IS.

So that's where you're coming from! And that's why you want to kick me when I'm down, and otherwise take things out on me. What are you taking out on me?
MAYBE THINGS THAT WERE TAKEN OUT ON ME!

This could be important. You are the critic, the judge, yet you are irritated and impatient with me. You are reacting to me, just as I react to you.
DID YOU THINK IT WAS OTHERWISE?

I guess I thought you would at least pretend to come from a more impartial place, the judge side of you, like weighing pros and cons, that kind of thing.
WELL, I TRY TO GIVE THAT IMPRESSION BUT IT DOESN'T ALWAYS HAPPEN THAT WAY. I GET VERY IMPATIENT WITH YOU. YOU ARE SO BLIND! SO STUPID!

Why do you call me stupid?
BECAUSE OF YOUR NAIVETÉ, YOUR INNOCENCE...IT'S IDIOTIC TO BE LIKE THAT. YOU'VE GOT TO BE TOUGH, UNBENDING, NO SLACKER, NO IDEALIST.

Other forms of tyranny flooded my dreams at night. Japanese, Nazis, soldiers and American Indians pursued, tortured or tried to murder me and my Hero. In the daytime, I could reason about all this inner violence. Perhaps my World War II childhood brought this on, I thought. I told myself these dreams had to be about repression or control—a refusal to admit to other aspects of myself. Or perhaps some unknown, unconscious energy wanted to force another part of me to submit to it. But such reasoning only worked during the day. At night a world I'd never acknowledged erupted, filled with brutality, arrogance, contempt and a murderous brilliance that refused to acknowledge weakness. I asked one murderer:

Why do you hate me so? You are a part of me, an unredeemed part. How can I make a relation with you and your violence?
THERE'S NO EXCUSE!

But I have a body that gets tired.
RE-ANIMATE IT.

Sometimes I have to accept my limitations.
FAH!

Without this body you wouldn't exist.
I'D FIND ANOTHER WAY.

To do what?
TO AFFIRM THE BEST. TO BE THE BEST.

Oh, so you are a 'winner?'
THAT'S WHAT I DO BEST.

But what do you win? And is it worth killing for?
YOU HAVE YOUR GOALS. I HAVE MINE.

But we are one person, sometimes torn in two by your murderous anger.
I WILL SUCCEED!

At what cost?
AT ALL COSTS!!!

Why were these negative figures so scornful? Desperate to find out, I asked the Tyrant:

Where is this harsh attitude coming from?
I'M TENSE.

Are you afraid? Why do you have to tear down, never build up?
I SEE THROUGH THE NONSENSE TO THE HEART OF THE MATTER.

There is no heart in what you do. It does violence to feeling.
I SEE WHAT IS AND I CALL IT LIKE I SEE IT.

No. You grind my nose in the dirt or stab me in the back with a surprise attack. Why? What are you trying to make up for?
ALL THE BLINDNESS AND INADEQUACY! THERE ARE JUST NO STANDARDS ANY MORE.

How about children...why humiliate, punish, hurt, frighten and otherwise abuse them? Why not teach them, lead them, assist them?
BLIND FOOLS!

How can they learn if you scare them? Your presence is like a four-alarm fire or a knife in the dark. Who can learn anything from that but to fear you? How can I hear you when you produce such fear?
I LIKE THE RESPECT IT BRINGS. IT GIVES ME SOME CLASS!

These early exchanges seemed to increase my reflux pain. One morning I woke up feeling sick to my stomach, my hand on my solar plexus and the words, "the field of Cain," ringing in my

ears. How was I the field of Cain, who murdered his own brother?
Would a dialogue help?

Why do you attack me?
BECAUSE YOU'RE STUPID! YOU DIDN'T LOOK FAR ENOUGH. YOU ALWAYS MISS THE MARK!

Why don't you help instead of attacking?
YOU AREN'T WORTH THE TROUBLE.

That's not a reason. You're part of me.
THE BEST PART.

Maybe so, but then you should help. Is there any way we could work together?
MILES APART.

Could I learn from you?
THAT'S BETTER. NOW YOU'RE TALKING MY LANGUAGE. TAKE A BACK SEAT AND LET ME RUN THE SHOW.

That wouldn't work either. In fact, I believe we already tried that. Do you have any other suggestions?
LEARN FROM THOSE BETTER AND STRONGER THAN YOU. I'M ALWAYS CLEAR WHAT I WANT. YOU ALWAYS HESITATE.

I hesitate because I want to do what's best, what's right.
BEST. RIGHT. THAT'S WHAT I'M IN CHARGE OF!

　　Here I was, trying to do my best to be a decent human being. Yet this judgmental, negative energy lived somewhere inside me. From the Tyrant's point of view, I never worked fast enough or hard enough. My to-do list became endless. Sometimes it seemed like a load of bricks falling on me, battering me down. At other moments a punishing presence seemed to sit on my head, pressing me so I could barely breathe.

One day, after the Tyrant attacked me for not getting enough done when I'd scarcely slept the night before, I cried: *"This is just too much! Why must I fill every waking minute with achievement? Why can't I just be alive to myself without doing, doing, doing?"*

Why do you always attack me?
YOU'RE ATTACKABLE.

Where do you come from in my life?
YOUR BROTHER, YOUR MOTHER, YOUR FATHER, YOUR STEPFATHER. NAME IT AND YOU'VE GOT IT. OH, AND DON'T FORGET GOOD OLD MISS P. !

At heart, what are you accusing me of?
OF NOT BEING GOOD ENOUGH. YOU CAN'T MAKE IT. YOU LOSE, YOU LOSER!

Why are you in such a hurry for me to get things done?
TO FEEL BETTER.

Don't you see how I pay a price for you feeling better?

But wait a minute! Could his last comment mean these conversations were getting somewhere? Perhaps if I felt better I could be free of him. I tried acupuncture to relieve the pain, and for a day or two he was gone. But it didn't help me get through my to-do list. No ambition to do anything, no interest in getting myself going. My projects and activities lay untouched. I sat down again to write, in search of help. But the minute I admitted how lost I felt,

the Tyrant was back, condemning my confusion. Discouraged, I
opened a new dialogue:

Why do you hate me so? Why do you attack me so?
WHO'S ATTACKING WHO?

I thought it was obvious but maybe it isn't. Can you shed some
light?
IN ORDER TO AVOID BEING ATTACKED YOU HAVE TO
ATTACK. CRITICIZING PUTS YOU ON ANOTHER LEVEL,
ABOVE THE OTHER FELLA. SCORN DOES THE SAME.

Is there a way we could live together, inhabiting the same body,
and not destroying it or each other? What's the common
denominator between us? I've expressed my view of you. Why
don't you say exactly how you feel about me?
YOU ARE STUPID, NAIVE, BUMBLING, INADEQUATE,
IDIOTIC.

Ouch. Here we go again!

Nevertheless, something new was happening inside. As I
described it in my journal: *A new feeling of space comes between*
my present state and my next project. For the first time, I can dare
to change my plans at the last minute. But each time I do, I feel the
powerful presence of someone who wants me to remain on a rigid
schedule. This is definitely not my fussy alter ego, Mrs. Rigid, but a
powerful male force determined to keep me on track.

NO DIVERGING FROM THE ORIGINAL ORDERS 'FROM
ABOVE.'
Wow! Who are you?

THE ONE WHO KNOWS.
How do you know?

I'VE THOUGHT IT OUT.
Why is no change to be allowed?

BECAUSE THAT MIGHT UPSET THINGS.
What would it upset?

THE DIVINE ORDER OF HOW IT SHOULD BE.
But it's just a plan!

TO YOU, MAYBE. TO ME IT BECOMES LAW.
So each plan becomes set in stone?

THAT'S RIGHT. IT HAS VALUE BECAUSE I THOUGHT IT OUT.
What's the value of impulse?

CHILDISH. WEAK. DEVIANT. POWER IS IN STICKING TO THE PLAN.

No room for spontaneity there! Clearly my Tyrant thought his orders were absolute law. But how could these unforgiving rules be my own? And above all, how could I possibly escape from them? I felt overwhelmed, helpless. What could satisfy this inexorable judge? Suddenly, a prayer blossomed like a flower in my heart: *May I find the way to relate to this disciplinarian.* So I asked:

Disciplinarian, are you here, available to talk?
THAT DEPENDS WHAT IT'S ABOUT. IS IT USEFUL? MEANINGFUL?

I hope so. I need to know you better. What do you want to tell me?
I'M CLEAR HEADED AND CLEAR THINKING AND YOU MUDDLE THINGS TOO MUCH. THAT'S WHY YOU NEED ME AROUND TO STRAIGHTEN YOU OUT.

Is there a way to help me, rather than stabbing, beating or otherwise attacking me?
I'LL THINK ABOUT IT. MAYBE THAT DEPENDS ON YOU.

How can I help get us to that place where we can exchange?
LISTEN MORE. AND SOMETIMES BE GUIDED.

Why do you want to hurt me?
IT'S THE ONLY WAY TO GET YOU TO PAY ATTENTION?

I hear a question in that answer, which gives me hope. I'd like to find a way to work with you, rather than our opposing each other. You said I never listen. It's true. I'm too busy. But what am I not listening to? Can you clarify?
YOU TAKE OVER RIGHT AWAY. YOU CALL ME A TYRANT BUT YOU ARE VERY, VERY BOSSY!

Maybe I've had to summon up bossiness and stop listening because I've been so afraid of you.
WHAT'S TO BE AFRAID OF?

Surely you're joking! I cringe when you come after me with your whiplash tongue and your words like stabbing knives. I'm a prisoner of fear, of rigidity. I'm afraid of change. How could we work together? You see things so clearly, yet you always attack me after things have happened. Couldn't you remind me earlier sometimes?
YOU NEVER LISTEN!

YOU, TOO, HAVE AN INNER TYRANT

That's my story, but Tyrant energy exists in all of us. Its power resides in our fear of anything that threatens the status quo or requires a new attitude. Proceed with caution in your encounters with him, because he can wound what's delicate and sensitive in you. His messages have real elements of truth but are twisted by a point of view that sees everything in black-or-white negatives.

RULE NUMBER ONE: LEARN TO LISTEN

In spite of the fact that the Tyrant loved to cut me down, his repeated accusation that I never listened offered me a daily task. I began to tune in to all kinds of inner comments of which I'd previously been unaware. I'd assumed they were 'my' thoughts and I was one single, indivisible person. But it became clear that there were many points of view in me.

WHO ARE YOU, REALLY?

While my experiences with him revealed two opposing sides, each trying to defend herself from the other, I began to doubt whether either of them was "the real me." Perhaps your own persona figures are like my Tyrant, Frightened Child, and Mrs. Rigid—simply actors in your cast of characters, fragments thrown up by the drama of your life.

THE TYRANT IS ALL ABOUT CONTROL

He maintains our illusion that if we hold on tight we'll be better off. Life taught us early that mistakes are dangerous and we must hide them. But as Robert Johnson pointed out in Living Your Unlived Life, "The road to strength is vulnerability and openness. Mistakes are absolutely essential. Unfortunately, we learn in school that mistakes are something to fear, hide, or avoid."

DON'T LET HIM FLAY YOU WITH ACCUSATIONS

Get to know the Tyrant's vocabulary. Above all, down with 'oughts' and 'shoulds!' Be alert to when you hear yourself say, "I ought to have..." to yourself; or "you definitely should..." to someone else. Instead, sing the chorus of David Roth's song from *Rising in Love* to your Tyrant: "Don't 'should' on me and I won't 'should' on you!"

IT'S NOT EASY TO BE OPEN AND VULNERABLE
This isn't something you can force. In my case, a gradual opening to these unconscious energies took place over a long time. My attitude began to shift when, as a result of paying attention to dreams and dialogues I didn't understand, the physical pain began to recede along with the emotional anguish, at least for a little while. This gave me the courage to continue the investigation.

THERE'S ALWAYS SOMETHING TO LEARN
A message lurks behind the words and images but the form it takes is often confusing. The unconscious seems to love to make jokes or play on words. It over-exaggerates and is especially good at double meanings. If you can accept that it speaks a different language, you're halfway to the right approach. What's important then, and at all times, is to continue to listen.

YOU MAY FEEL YOU BOTH 'GET IT' AND DON'T GET IT
Something may tug at your understanding but you can't quite put it into words. Relax and continue to listen rather than trying to figure it all out. Your gut can tell you more about the Tyrant than your head. Reread your notes. Replay the dream or the dialogue. Listen to it with your body and your feeling reactions.

TALK RESPECTFULLY TO THE TYRANT
This isn't a game and the dynamic energy represented by the Tyrant has a great deal of power. As you ask what you need to know, listen carefully to the answers. Be honest and authentic and he will return the favor, although not necessarily to your liking. Nevertheless, be sure to treat him with respect. It's important to remember that the more unconscious you are of this energy or the more you deny its existence, the more power it has over you.

Thirteen: Pursued by Hungry Ghosts

"Do not be afraid, do not be attracted to the soft yellow light of the hungry ghosts. That is the light-path of unconscious tendencies accumulated by your intense desire. If you are attracted to it you will fall into the realm of hungry ghosts and experience unbearable misery from hunger and thirst."
Tibetan Book of the Dead (Chogyam Trungpa translation).

We seldom think about death until we're faced with it—upsetting news about friends or family, or the ultimate threat to our own lives. I was more or less immune to such worries until my aging mother's memory and my stepfather's once keen eyesight began to fade. Putting further pressure on my work schedule, I hastened to fit in walks in the park for her and a visit to the Lighthouse for him. At the same time, my birth father's prostate cancer became more active. I struggled to support their final years as I tried to confront my own mortality. How to find an inner resolution to the questions it raised?

Their deaths within two years of each other toppled the unstable balance I'd achieved. My stepfather left us after a dramatic ten-day hospital marathon—family and friends accompanying him around the clock. My father suffered a long, painful decline that ended exactly a year later. Mother left us on Christmas Day, a year after that.

While I was grieving, a pocket edition of the *Tibetan Book of the Dead* caught my eye in a bookstore. I remembered how she had poured over it years before so I bought it and began to read avidly. Ostensibly, it serves as a Buddhist guidebook to accompany the dying through their final earthly ordeal. In one edition, Robert Thurman translates the title as *The Great Book of Liberation through Understanding in the Between.* He explains that there are other "betweens" besides the one that links the moment when dying begins and the final death of the body. For example, there's also the space between birth and dying—our life on earth. Such an approach invites us to think in terms of process rather than finality. From that point of view, the book is also a guide to living in the present as we try to free ourselves from the prison of our turning thoughts and our reactive nature.

The format is that of a friend or relative who whispers messages into the dying person's ear, advising him or her on how to meet the many deities who will now try to claim the soul between the moment dying "begins" and the time it passes on to another world. To alert the soul to oncoming challenges, the guide describes the apparitions who will try to persuade him, her (or us) to follow them. Wrathful and peaceful divinities compete to tempt the soul away from the help that's available from a higher level. We learn that while the true gods dazzle with their bright light and seem more frightening, the soul must welcome them in spite of their awesome nature. Otherwise the soft, inviting hellish gods will tempt us into their mesh.

The "Hungry Ghosts" had visited me long before I read about them in *The Book of the Dead*. The descriptions reminded me of certain familiar emotional states that drained me of energy. They hovered like ghostly presences in my psychic life. Robert Johnson, in *Living Your Unlived Life*, drew a comparison between the ancient Greek world of Hades, "where souls stirred amid the unchanging, redundant, disembodied, 'dead' weight of the past," and the modern concept of complexes: "unconscious figures that are colorless, repetitive, and separated from the dynamic flow of life."

Since Trungpa's edition fit right into my pocket, I took it everywhere as I struggled to understand my pain and fear. The guide's words offered a new approach to the ebb and flow of my emotional reactions: "O Child, whatever you see, however terrifying it is, recognize it as your own projection; recognize it as the luminosity, the natural radiance of your own mind."

"That's it," I sighed. "My personal Hungry Ghosts are inner attitudes that sap my strength and joy of living." Perhaps if I could acknowledge how they attract me with their neediness, and see in them my own longings, jealousies and desires for approbation, I'd take a step toward inner freedom. I tried to think of them as dangerous representatives of the complexes that imprisoned me and wondered whether, if I became more conscious of them and their insatiable hunger, they wouldn't be able to "eat" me as they did.

What if I found names for them in the same way I'd worked with my personas? Immediately a series of adjectives swarmed into my head like buzzing bees: *relentless, tyrannical, justifying, competing, judgmental, disapproving, inadequate, fearful.* Wow! Why would I want to live dominated by such nasty creatures? And why did I work so hard to satisfy them? For example, why accept the Slave-driver, a familiar daytime apparition who drove me daily beyond my normal limits. I saw myself jump into action when he cracked his whip even after his pushing and pressing had used up my energy.

These ghostly presences also lived in my dreams, relentless and unforgiving, in the guise of a host of spies, murderers, a Nazi torturer and a Savage who cut me into pieces. Did they enjoy what they put me through? I saw the Nazi smile as he twisted his knife in the Hero's wounds, but the Savage was somehow different. He came from a natural world and followed its laws, although he seemed to be always angry as he chopped me up into body parts. Perhaps I needed to learn what he was raging about. In any case, my innocence and trust were ravaged by all of them. I was a prisoner of their violence.

If what my Jungian guides said was true, that violence had to be in me. It was my energy that drove these negative personas. So I asked myself, "Why do I do what I do? What motivates me to act?" The answer came in three D's: Duty, Desire and Distrust.

Could the Tyrant represent an exaggerated call to duty and the Savage the expression of natural desires? I approve, authorize and feel good about "doing my duty." But what do I deny myself? If I were freer of self-restrictions, would the Savage be less violent? Would the murderers disappear?

If I were to escape this division between duty and desire, whom could I trust? Marion Woodman wrote in *The Ravaged Bridegroom*: "Perfectionism and blind duty can ravage a woman's body, spirit, emotions, relationships, self-respect, self-care and equanimity. As a goal, perfection is usually lethal because it is never met and our failure leaves us with the pain of comparison. And doing one's duty is empty and soul-withering unless it is fed by love."

Lethal, indeed! Under attack from destructive duty in the guise of the Tyrant and blind perfectionism attached to my Good Girl and Little Friend of All the World persona, how could I escape? I queried a dream murderer who'd waited for me in the shadows:

Why do you want to kill me? Have you no feeling?
WHAT DO YOU CARE? YOU JUST DO YOUR THING AND PAY NO ATTENTION.

I'm trying to understand why you are there and what your presence is telling me. Why do you kill?
DO YOU THINK ANYONE WOULD NOTICE ME IF I DIDN'T?

But why do you want to be noticed?
I HAVE A RIGHT TO MY TWO CENTS JUST LIKE ANYONE ELSE.

Can't you tell me what it is you want to get across so I can digest it better?

WHO LISTENS? NOT YOU!!

But what part of me do you want to murder?
WHAT DO YOU THINK, YOU JERK! THE PART THAT DOESN'T LISTEN TO ME!!!

Astonished, I asked myself what wasn't I listening to? Would my inner situation change if I honored these ghosts in some way? After all, they contain my energy and fuel my life. Duty deserves respect even if, in my case, it was tyrannical. As for savage needs and desires, surely they must be taken into account. But how to avoid getting cut to pieces? Perhaps the sufferer of these murderous attacks could reveal an answer:

You who feel pressured, confused and off-base when I'm in a hurry, what do you fear?
THERE'S NO ROOM FOR ME WHEN YOU'RE IN A HURRY. YOU MAKE ME SQUEEZE MYSELF INTO A SMALL SPACE TO KEEP OUT OF YOUR WAY SO YOU CAN DO WHAT YOU HAVE TO DO. AND ON TOP OF THAT YOU GET MAD AT ME EVEN WHEN I'M TRYING TO KEEP OUT OF YOUR WAY!!!

That pronouncement prompted a new consultation with my Tyrant:

Whom do I have to make myself smaller for, squeeze myself out of the way for?
YOU MEAN, WHO'S IN CHARGE?

Can't I just be myself?
IF YOU WERE JUST YOURSELF YOU WOULD BE SO BORING AND ORDINARY AND STUPID NO ONE WOULD WANT YOU AROUND.

I guess I need an outside authority to tell me what's the Right thing to do because I can't take the chance of being wrong. I've been wrong so many times. Wrong equals Danger.
DANGER FROM WHOM OR WHAT?

Danger of being scorned, humiliated, exposed as a fool. To be wrong also equals shame...the finger pointed at you, mocking laughter.
RESPECT YOUR RIGIDITY. YOU NEED TO HOLD ON, TO KEEP YOURSELF TOGETHER, MAINTAIN FORM, HAVE ANSWERS. DON'T DESPISE YOURSELF FOR THAT.

What about the gun in my dreams? Who's pointing it at me? Who's always threatening me? I'm so afraid!
WHY SO MUCH FEAR?

There's so much I should be doing...
DOWN WITH OUGHTS AND SHOULDS! ASK YOURSELF NOT 'WHAT OUGHT I TO DO?' BUT WHAT'S INTELLIGENT, HERE AND NOW. ASK NOT 'HOW SHOULD I BE FEELING?' AND 'WHAT SHOULD I BE DOING?' BUT 'HOW DO I FEEL RIGHT NOW AND WHAT AM I DOING RIGHT NOW?'

I feel guilty all the time. I ended my dream of family by leaving Peru. I destroyed my children's 'nest' and haven't been able to offer them a satisfactory substitute here.
FACE THE GUILT ABOUT LEAVING YOUR HUSBAND AND BREAKING UP THE FAMILY. ACCEPT THEIR SUFFERING. THEY WOULDN'T HAVE EXISTED IF YOU HADN'T MARRIED HIM, WITH ALL THE PROBLEMS AND CHALLENGES THAT THEY AND YOU HAVE TODAY. LET YOUR ATTENTION BE ON THEM, NOT ON THEIR PROBLEMS, INADEQUACIES AND FEARS. IT IS THEY TO

WHOM YOU ARE RELATED. THE REST OF THE PACKAGE IS INEVITABLE!

As I continued to dialogue with these ghostly personas over months and years, they began to take on a less threatening shape and my physical pain lessened. The Tyrant often softened into Mrs. Critical Attitude, annoyed at me, but not quite so scathing, not so condemning. One day, I became present to her at the very moment she took me over. Suddenly aware that her negativity was separate from my true self, I recognized it as a contamination of my emotional state. Although I'd have dearly loved to wipe her out then and there, I was powerless to change the annoyance she expressed through me. Here I was, conscious of her machinations even as they rose up in me but unable to change my negative attitude. At least I wasn't completely sucked in to it!

Here's how it happened: I was at a small class of Alexander teachers, feeling really tired. I'd signed up for it and hoped to learn something, however the teacher aggravated me right from the start. Perhaps it was just bad chemistry but she seemed plaintive to my critical mind and unable to answer my questions. And each time I demanded explanations, she, herself, became irritated. While we knew we annoyed each other, both of us were experts at maintaining a civilized front. What's more, Mrs. Critical Attitude knew well how to be nasty even when she seemed polite! As I became aware of this new persona manifesting through me, my interest awakened. I even wondered to myself whether I ought to take this woman's class again, just to find out why she irritated me so!

"WASTE OF TIME!" shouts Mrs. C.A. into my inner ear, bristling at the idea. *"SHE DOESN'T KNOW WHAT SHE'S TALKING ABOUT!"* Well, maybe she does, another voice in me answered, but she doesn't know how to present it.

I realized this new experience was another taste of Jung's "holding the tension between the opposites"—becoming conscious of manifestations originating in the unconscious. I'd also heard it spoken of many times in the Gurdjieff work as the battle between 'yes' and 'no,' although I didn't connect the two formulations until later. Madame de Salzmann used to call it "staying in front of the lack." In the recently published *Reality of Being*, crafted from her private journal, she wrote: "If at the moment the opposing force appears I see in what the negation consists, I can wish to stay between the two thresholds and, by a special effort, come to separate the elements that feed off this negative emotion...I stay in front, accepting the friction between the 'yes' and the 'no."

That night I dreamt I was driving a truck very fast through a narrow alley. I'd miscalculated its width so the truck scraped against both sides and the alley walls began to crumble. Although I was safe inside as the walls turned into rubble, why was my truck energy forcing itself through such a narrow road? Did I need to find a wider path? Could I give up my tendency to a narrow focus?

From time to time, other ghosts and mysterious energies played through my dreams, but the most terrifying apparition came after a last performance of Mozart's Requiem with a group of singers in Prague one summer. It led me to a huge new truth: *We're spending the night in a kind of hostel, many of us sleeping in the same big room. A ghostly white figure appears for a moment near my bed. I'm filled with fear at this apparition whose long robes are full of patches, so that, in places, I can see right through her. I crawl to a private room, lock the door and fall back to sleep. Suddenly the same ghostly white presence appears again, wraith-like and wispy. I'm terrified and scream at her, "But the door was locked so you can't get in here!"*

My own scream woke me up and left me trembling. Unable to erase the wispy image or the fear I felt on seeing her, I wanted desperately to know why parts of her were missing. Just before we flew back to the U.S., I asked her:

Who are you, white specter?

PART OF YOU.

What are you here to remind me of?
WHAT YOU ARE LEAVING OUT.

Why am I so afraid?
ITS HARD TO ADMIT WHAT YOU'VE LOST OR FORGOTTEN OR NOT INCLUDED.

What are you trying to remind me of?
I AM A DISEMBODIED SPIRIT.

I think I'm trying too hard to get you to explain yourself. Are you a spirit of the past or the future?
I AM PRESENCE.

Are you saying you're always with me but I don't know it?
EXACTLY.

      The image of that wispy white ghost haunted me for weeks. Were the holes in her garment parts of myself I didn't accept or hadn't seen or couldn't admit to? Tearfully, I asked myself "Is this the unlived life I've heard about? Is it too late to understand what I've left out of my life, what I'm here for, what my task is?" Finally I dared another dialogue with her:

Wraithlike spirit, speak to me and tell me what it is I need to know. Are you there to help me?
DO YOU FEEL IN NEED OF HELP?

Very much. I no longer know what desires to trust, what judgments to listen to.
I COULD BE MORE WHOLE.

Is that good for me?
WHY NOT?

I don't know. Who are you?
PART OF YOURSELF.

Part that can help me?
YOU NEED TO ACCESS MORE OF YOURSELF. THAT INCLUDES ME.

Where can help come from?
FROM YOURSELF!

What mode should I live in? How can I learn from your presence?
MY PRESENCE ASKS A QUESTION YOU NEED TO ASK OF YOURSELF.

What question?
WHO AM I?

A few days later, I had a deeply meaningful dream: *I have to go into a dark cave in an unknown land, in magic ground. Something very precious is there but I have to give up knowing what I'm looking for and, above all, give up possessing it. But how? A new force suddenly moves in to help me so I'm able to go safely through the difficult and frightening experience. I find what is precious in the cave and then surrender it when I come out. Then I'm made love to by this force—totally helpless and open to it, passively allowing it to enter me without being able to oppose it. As the dream ends a voice says: "The difficulty is in taking responsibility for the treasure."*

MEET WITH YOUR OWN HUNGRY GHOSTS
See if you can catch a glimpse of these forces that drive you where you may not want to go. Perhaps it will only be out of the corner of your inner eye, because they really don't want to be discovered. That's a threat to their power over you. So resolve to take a step back from your emotional reactions at the end of each day. Begin to write about them in your notebook at night, when the soul becomes more quiet and reflective because your daily supply of energy has been largely used up.

WHAT DO THEY DO WITH YOUR ENERGY?
Make note of any strong feelings you have about what's going on in your life. See how you express them. Some people take action against perceived opposition with dire threats or shouts of wrath, while others may go to the other extreme and close down their receptivity to the world in order not to be hurt. Your personal Ghosts may express themselves in either of those two extremes or anywhere in between.

ADMIT TO YOUR HELPLESSNESS
I find I'm most helped when I admit I'm desperate. It may seem counter-intuitive, but giving up is a powerful tool that allows us to discover what's really going on. If these are huge, archetypal energies blowing through me, I'm safest when I'm in touch with my own limitations and the small piece of earth I occupy.

INVITE YOUR ACQUAINTANCES TO A MIND-PARTY
The people who annoy us most can be most helpful in our quest. Imagine a gathering of friends and acquaintances, fellow workers, the guy in the deli who always talks back, etc. Imagine conversations with them, or remember past encounters. Try to engage with each person/image and pinpoint what irritates you most about them. Write it down.

START A DIALOGUE WITH A MARGINAL PERSONA
Just as I did with Mrs. R, choose a member of your cast of characters who's not so dominant that you think of it as "you." It's hard to scope them out when we don't really want to admit to their existence, but well worth the attempt. One way to uncover them is to listen carefully to ourselves when we say or think, "I'm not like that!" or "That's not me!" Or even, with sorrowful pride, "That's just how I am and I can't change! Everyone will have to accept me as I am!"

WE MUST SOMETIMES ACCEPT WHAT SEEMS UNACCEPTABLE
Jung invited us to look deep into another level of psyche: "In each of us there is another we do not know. He speaks to us in dreams and tells us how differently he sees us from the way we see ourselves." And again, "We have in all naiveté forgotten that beneath our world of reason another lies buried." (MDR)

GET READY FOR SURPRISES
Don't assume an outcome. That's primary to learning something new. Prepare to be shocked. And don't cut off the exchange with a persona just because it says what you don't want to hear. Ask for clarification instead. If you can hold back strong reactions and really listen, or allow your reaction to morph into questioning words, you're sure to discover something.

TRY TO BE OPEN WITH EACH PERSONA/GHOST
Always approach a dialogue with care. Accept the uncertainty of the outcome. It's necessary to give up your in-charge persona for a little while, otherwise you're setting yourself up for disappointment. Our personas may not respond to closed minds or challenging attitudes. Why should they? After all, how many know-it-alls would you want to open up to?

GROUNDING OURSELVES CAN HELP US DEAL WITH GHOSTS

There's a reality in our own flesh and blood that brings us back to earth when we are confronted by ghostly voices. Marion Woodman recommended that we look to our own body-being for help: " Men as much as women need to know that their soul is grounded in their own loving matter. 'This is who I am. Every cell in my body tells me this is of value to me—not to my persona, to me.' That is the container whose feeling can be trusted because it is grounded in reality." (*The Ravaged Bridegroom*)

Fourteen: Woman in a Coma

The 'unconscious,' that which we don't know, is too often also the 'unloved,' that which we do not accept...We not only need to know more about ourselves, we also need to love more of ourselves...We need to be close to the movements of soul that run deep and yet have everything to do with the way we act and feel in life."
Thomas Moore, *Soul Mates*

The negative dynamics of my inner tyrants and terrorists riveted my attention for years. While their dramatic messages shook me deeply, I seldom thought about the feminine side of my nature. Surely depressed and terrorized parts of me must lie hidden there. I now felt it was urgent to bring these unattended parts into closer communication with my conscious awareness. But how? Could I face what my conscious self obviously avoided? Could I find the courage to listen to messages I didn't want to hear?

Gurdjieff often spoke about our inner buffers, like buffers on railway carriages or blinders on a horse, which protect us from seeing different or opposing aspects of ourselves. He recommended that we bring our conscious mind face to face with sides of ourselves that contradicted each other. I now realized that whenever I felt pain I buffered myself against what was happening. I'd find a book to read, take a walk, bury myself in one or another project.

"Bury myself." What an image! Did I really say that? Who's buried when I'm busy? As Jung said in *Man and His Symbols*, "Modern man protects himself against seeing his own split state by a system of compartments. Certain areas of outer life and of his own behavior are kept, as it were, in separate drawers and are never confronted with one another...the sad truth is that man's real life consists of a complex of inexorable opposites—day and night, birth and death, happiness and misery, good and evil...Life is a battleground, and if it were not so, existence would come to an end."

One morning I felt slowed down, even stopped. Although I was expert at how to gear up, to drive myself to "feel better," I decided to let go into this slowed-down-ness to see what it could teach me. The effort didn't last long. By noon the familiar habit of shaking myself into action had taken over. I went to the park to practice Tai Chi and acquire more yang energy, but when I caught sight of the changed dynamic I decided to take a short walk instead. That led to a major discovery: why did I think the yang mode, which I prefer, is more "centered" than the yin mode? Yes, it's more comfortable for me to feel clearheaded, energetic and body-powered, so it makes sense to push myself into that state. But pushing is yang. Receiving is yin. They represent two extremes. Both are necessary to live a more balanced life.

Back home I lunched, lay down and slept heavily. I woke up feeling afraid. Had I been wrong not to push myself onto the "better" path of action, in spite of resistance? I asked for help:

Somebody please assure me I made the right move and wasn't just lazy. Where does my true freedom lie?
Freedom is freedom from yes and no.

But aren't I supposed to meet and conquer resistance?
Who resists? Who forces?

But isn't it better for me-as-a-whole to be pushed into the better action when I'm tired?
What action is that?

The one that's better for me in general, like swimming, taking a walk, or doing Tai Chi.

Who's in charge?

Does it matter?
What do _you_ think?

Feeling good is better than feeling bad. Activity is better than passivity.
Who is passive when you push yourself around? And who is active when you force yourself?

   Hmm. Good question. When, a few days later, I was overwhelmed by a deep inner anguish, I ventured a dialogue with the unknown sufferer:

There's weeping going on in me. Please tell me who you are.
I'm hurt and afraid, hurt and afraid.

I want to help and comfort you, to find a way to ease your pain.
O hurt, hurt, hurt, the whole world hurts. The whole world is in pain. My children hurt, my parents hurt, my friends hurt and people hurt each other when they are in pain.

So what can we do but bear the pain we feel? Can anything help?
Not to run away, not to bury yourself in activity or reading books. Don't refuse to see the pain or the fatigue that hides emotional denial. Let the river run!!!

O.K. I'm here. I choose to be here. I choose to feel the pain. I won't turn away or hide behind books or doing stuff.
I am here, too.

Dear hurt and frightened one, you must be cared for, protected and loved.

This dialogue pointed my attention to the vague, unpleasant moods I'd always tried to talk myself out of before. I went to the park to practice Tai Chi under a tree. It was a rainy day, so not many people were around. I liked that—me alone with the universe. But when I was halfway through, someone walked by. Out of the corner of my eye I saw him stare at me. An almost inaudible inner voice muttered, *"I'm only safe when I'm alone."* When I got home, I asked:

Who's that who is only safe alone? Are you there?
Of course. I'm always here.

Why are you so afraid?
How do I know? I only know I can breathe more freely, and think my own thoughts only when there's nobody around.

You mean you can't even think private thoughts when someone else is there?
That's right. I have to think about <u>them</u>. Yesterday the phone rang while I was putting a bandage on my knee and I forgot to rinse the cut.

So maybe it's a question of attention? You don't have attention for two things?
I don't have attention for me! I don't have the right to think about me when I'm with someone else.

Can I convince you that I will try to take care of you?
You? What can you do? You can't even take care of yourself!!!

But somewhere there's a protector. There has to be. Like superman when we were little.
But superman is imaginary. He doesn't exist and he doesn't help.

Well, how about the inner masculine? Someone's got to care about you. And me.

The inner masculine spends all his time being angry. That's no help at all!

Well, I wish to find a way for us. I care for my cat, Gatsby, and you are delicate and subtle and gentle like Gatsby, aren't you?

I don't know what I am. Just that I'm afraid when other people are around. They cut me, they absorb me, they ignore me, they scorn me, but they don't even see me!

A door began to open to a whole world of grief inside me, pain I'd never allowed myself to feel. Between Superman and the Hero I'd been able to keep it closed: "Set my leg, coach, and give me the ball" had been my joking reference to how I dealt with hardship. But when a close friend died, as I grieved her premature death from cancer, the sudden fear of my own decline invaded me. I cried out:

Is old age finally catching up with me? I forget names, words, and sometimes wonder, "What did I come into this room for, anyway?"
STOP DOING SO MUCH!

Now you are angry at me because I didn't want to go for a swim today. Why?
I THINK IF YOU JUST PULLED IT TOGETHER AND GOT ON TRACK YOU WOULD FEEL A LOT BETTER.

You may be right. But how could I know whether I needed the rest? Am I lazy?
OF COURSE YOU ARE! WHAT A QUESTION!

Well maybe our exchange will be more useful if I ask another kind of question. How can we work together so life isn't a battle between us?
WHAT'S TO WORRY? LIVELY DISCUSSION IS PART OF THE GAME.

This doesn't feel like a game. It's not lively discussion when you're punishing me and making me feel bad for not doing what you think I should do.
LIVELY FOR ME THOUGH. STIRS UP THE JUICES!

I'm not here to stir up your juices! I want to stand on my own two feet and be authentic and do what's needed for balance between mind and body. You are a part of that and should work with me.
HEY! WAIT A MINUTE! I'M A FRAGMENT, NOT A PARTICIPANT. I'M A PIECE OF THE MACHINERY. LAY OFF THE BUDDY-BUDDY STUFF!

But a dialogue is needed between mind/thought of what's good for me and body or what I feel like doing.
THAT'S THREE PARTS NOT TWO.

You're right. I hadn't seen it clearly. I need to factor in my feelings.

Once more an acrimonious dialogue pointed me toward a new perspective. Feelings. I had marginalized major "feeling" issues or refused to admit them into my experiments. I lived in two modes—the wish to accomplish something and the wish to be— and they constantly warred with each other. I'd battle against physical fatigue to finish something, or turn away from my busness to rest and ponder. The former required that I stick to a plan of action come hell or high water, the latter meant that I must relinquish all plans in order to discover what was going on at a deeper level. That's when feeling would appear. That's when I'd often run back into "doing." Could I stay with it instead? Could I suffer it?

Since I was on my way to Florida to visit my father at that time, I determined to be more sensitive to my feelings for a few days. But at the very first attempt to relinquish my usual plans and be present to what I felt, anxiety invaded me. I'd turn into a vegetable! I needed action, immediate commitments, in order to feel good about myself. So I queried my unknown helper:

Why am I afraid? How can I live more in balance?
Know whom you serve.

But when all is quiet, the body resting, the pulse of fear becomes clearer. I've got to keep going. I can't stop.
Why? It's time to take a break, chill out.

But if I stop I may fall apart, or become a vegetable and lie down forever.
Hey! What's a little rest, a little lie-down? It might help.

Yes, that's true, but if I only I can just keep going...
Where are you going?

To a better position? A better place to be? I'm swimming and walking on the beach to keep myself in top condition.
Oho! So you're moving along to top, top, top condition. But what happens as you get older and your body fails to be so very top, top?

I have no idea, but I want to put that off as long as possible!
So here's something to think about: Top condition at 65 may be different from 55 or 75. What's top condition made of?

I guess the basic concept is to feel good.

Through this exchange, my narrow viewpoint was illumined and widened yet again. As a result, my attitude toward pain and emotional suffering began to change. Sometimes, as "my stiff upper lip" softened, I stayed longer in states of suffering before trying to distract myself. It wasn't easy to stay in the pain rather than run away to clean the closets or scrub the kitchen floor. One day, as I sat quietly in an attempt to accept the anguish that had surged up out of nowhere, a sudden realization filled me: *I AM THE PORTAL! And only through this portal can I connect with the meaning of my life.*

I summoned up courage to accept any messages hidden behind the pain. But how could I admit to my weakness without a backlash from the Tyrant? He usually moved in to crush me whenever I felt vulnerable. Nevertheless, in spite of my feeling of helplessness, a shift in power was taking place. Deep in that foreign land below my mind, between the Doer—thinker, planner, controller—and the Receiver—the open portal—a new relationship was aborning.

Why had I been so fearful of this more open state? Because in it I felt confused, slow-moving, uncertain of what was going to happen. A few years before, I'd have declared, "If this is the portal to the unconscious, no way do I want to let it flood in and drown me, so I'd better get busy doing something right away!"

But as I continued to be more present to my fears, a part of me actively sought the portal. And the price of returning to this receptive mode was to stay with the pain and confusion rather than hurry away into doing stuff. As I wrote in my journal, *Part of me looks for what to do so as (1) not to waste time and (2) to push away the pain. The other side doesn't know what to do. But today I'm here between the two. I've chosen to be here, refused to go onto the next thing on my list. From moment to moment, I feel a tug from the side that's longing to escape into security by getting to work at something.* I decided to dialogue with the side that wanted to push me to action:

You the head, the organizer, the setter up of lists and the person who gets things done, how do you feel about what's going on right now?
There's a lot that could be done that isn't getting done. I always suffer when a free day is wasted without getting something done.

But what about this other, inner life? How can I know what I need? What do you think I need?
A path to follow; a practice to engage in. And you need to keep to it every day. Not so on-again, off-again Finnegan, depending on whether you feel like it or not.

But couldn't I be so busy with a path that I lose the present reality?
You wanted my opinion. I've given it to you. A drop of water that falls repeatedly on a rock will sooner or later create a pool.

How can we work together for the same end?
What stands in the way?

Forgetfulness. Forgetting the present reality, Perhaps remembering can only come through feeling.
I know nothing of feeling. But I know it's necessary.

Help me. Let's work together.
Is this another flash in the pan? How can I believe you mean it?

During this time of new discoveries my dreams began to change. Women often replaced the tyrants, cops and criminals. Instead of cringing under enemy attack, I vibrated with the panic of a fearful young girl chased by a drug dealer. What part of me was drugging myself and running away? And how could I stop running?

In another dream, an elderly woman fell down a short flight of stairs. Or did she just give up and collapse because life was too much for her? A third dream created an overwhelming sense of helplessness: *A female guard in a Nazi prison camp prepares a group of us for an ordeal. She has given each captured woman a number and we're taken to a laboratory to be part of an experiment. Although civil, she avoids our questions. We can't figure out what the experiment is but we know we're being used and won't come out of it alive.*

I woke from this dream with the ominous feeling of being under someone else's control. So I asked the woman:

What are we being used for?
I CAN'T TELL YOU.

Who are you…what part do you play?
I'M THE ORGANIZER.

Whom do you serve?
THE COLLECTIVE.

Why are you so imposing?
I CARRY A LOT OF WEIGHT.

Is there any way to escape?
THAT'S YOUR PROBLEM.

Do you have a name?
I AM LEGION.

My analyst called this a clear-cut expression of the inner tension between finding my way as an individual, and the collective influence on me of the world I lived in. Just as the persona opposes any changes to the status quo, this imposing woman gave no value to the individual life of these women but used them for experimental purposes. Under whose authority were we imprisoned? Under what conditions did I accept another authority than my own?

Although that dream was a shocker, worse was to come. My encounter with the Woman in a Coma shook me to my very depths: *A cruel and demanding man shoots a woman because of something she hasn't done. Perhaps she didn't move fast enough to do his bidding or perhaps she refused. Now she lies in a coma, bleeding to death, on a large table. No one is doing anything to get her help because everyone is afraid of the man who shot her. He tells them that as soon as he is given what he wants or some situation is reversed, he will let them take her to the hospital.*

I tried to figure the message out: the cruel masculine and the defenseless feminine must represent sides of myself. I'd already suspected I could be too passive. It was the opposite pole to my hyperactivity. But who was the gunman who would do anything to get what he wanted? Why was he holding the woman hostage? And what did he mean that some situation must be reversed? When I took the word reverse apart it became re-verse, which sounds like re-write. Was he pointing out that there's a story here that needs to be rewritten? If so, wow!

The next day I asked him why he was so angry. I expected him to shout at me but to my surprise, he whined:
NOBODY'S EVER THERE FOR ME! I CAN'T MAKE ANYONE HAPPY. GIRLS ARE HARD TO PLEASE. BUT IF I TAKE OVER, WHATEVER GOES WRONG IS ALWAYS MY FAULT!

Then I turned to the Woman in a Coma:

Woman, why do you lie there without any sign of life?
BECAUSE IF I MOVE I MIGHT GET CLOBBERED.

But you have rights!
NOT AGAINST THIS GUY. HE WON'T GIVE ME ANY SLACK.

What would happen if you tried to get up off the table and tell him what you feel?
HE'D BEAT ME UP.

Why can't you find someone to fight for you, to help you?
ALL THE MEN IN MY LIFE ARE LIKE THAT, ANGRY AND DEMANDING.

Then is there no solution to this impasse? Must you lie there forever?
I DON'T KNOW. SOMETHING NEEDS TO COME TO LIFE IN ME.

My analyst referred to the man as a power animus, an aggressive, hostile figure whose tyrannical drive for perfection lacked compassion for my neediness and vulnerability. In other words, my need to be perfect had taken on a murderous life of its own, refusing to accept any form of weakness, including my ordinary humanity.

Victim and victimizer represent a pair of opposites: power and vulnerability; loss of feeling to retain power and loss of power to affirm feeling. Where was the third, the other energy that was needed to resolve this unending internal combat? Since that comatose feminine seemed unable to defend herself, what could I do to save her?

ACCEPT INNER DIVISION

Jung said it best: "Conflict engenders fire, the fire of affects and emotions, and like every other fire it has two aspects, that of combustion and that of creating light. On the one hand, emotion is the alchemical fire whose warmth brings everything into existence and whose heat burns all superfluities to ashes. . . . But on the other hand, emotion is the moment when steel meets flint and a spark is struck forth, for emotion is the chief source of consciousness. There is no change from darkness to light or from inertia to movement without emotion." (CW 9)

ONLY GENTLENESS CAN DEAL WITH FEARFULNESS

Go gently into any effort at contacting what's hidden and afraid in you. To throw a frightened child into the water won't make it braver. It will probably just hate swimming for the rest of its life. So treat the fearful, escaping, avoiding, postponing part of yourself like a beloved child. Don't scold it. Love it, comfort it and encourage it to take more risks. Tell it you're there to help.

CHALLENGE THE ATTITUDE THAT LIFE IS AN ORDEAL

An ordeal is something that's done to you. You meet it passively, like my Woman in a Coma. Yes, life presents us with hardships we can do nothing about, but we can deal with them better if our attitude toward what overwhelms us becomes more conscious. And when we approach problems as challenges rather than ordeals, we meet what's inevitable in a more active way.

QUESTION REACTIONS, LOOK FOR RESPONSES

Reactions are usually repetitive and habitual, a pattern set in us long ago. Responses, on the other hand, come from a present, reasoned outlook. As you approach any effort to bring your shy inner self into a more active mode, avoid pressuring that young part of yourself. Ask yourself, how can a child deal with harsh demands? Instead, simply witness your own reactions, withdrawals, denials, hesitations. There are many ways of saying 'no' to life.

OPEN A DIALOGUE WITH WHAT'S COMATOSE OR AFRAID TO MOVE

Let kindness to yourself guide your efforts. As you listen carefully to fears and complaints, say, "Yes. I am here for you." As James Hollis reminded us in one of his recent books, Philo of Alexandria long ago said: "Be kind. Everyone you meet has a very large problem." Include yourself in that, because you and I also have very large problems! Let your mind stretch to put yourself in the other guy's shoes, including the Other in yourself.

NOW SPEAK TO THE ANGRY OR UNCARING OTHER SIDE

Begin with reasonable curiosity. What's that persona angry about? What's bugging him or her? Let the dialogue unfold as you listen carefully without arguing. Then bring questions you desperately need answers for into the conversation. Let that inner urgency to understand guide your words. And let it rule your effort to listen.

WHERE ARE YOU PASSIVE AND HOW COULD YOU BE MORE ACTIVE?

Withdrawing into passivity is an escape from reality. Nevertheless, sometimes one needs to stop trying to change one's life and curl up with a murder mystery (my solution) or a good movie. But in those moments of burning anguish, when nothing helps, explore an action that might bring a taste of freedom. Only you can know, or discover, what your personal act toward freedom is. It will probably be small, simple and feel somewhat like giving up control.

SMALL BEGINNINGS ARE MORE REAL

We wish we could change overnight, especially when we begin to realize how completely we've let ourselves down. But habitual attitudes are powerful. So as you approach a problematic persona or try to approach an important person in your life in a different way, it's better to undertake a small experiment. Remind yourself that the witness within you is a potent companion to your search.

THE BENEFIT OF THE DOUBT IS REAL, TOO

Give your outer partner or your problem inner persona more leeway, more respect. We need to listen to the other more than we have until now and let new information enter into the prison of our old habitual reactions. It may help the other, too. Remember, like creates like. Anger creates anger; openness invites openness in return. The unconscious reflects our attitude toward it, and so do other people. They will react to our openness or our annoyance in the same coin. Pay it forward.

Fifteen: The Lord of Discipline

No matter how sovereign we believe we are, we remain the lowliest of serfs to the tyrannies of whatever remains unconscious."

James Hollis, *What Matters Most*

The Woman in a Coma called me to a new task: to reconcile the hypercritical masculine Tyrant I harbored with my fearful feminine side. I now realized it was relationship issues with fathers and husband that had left me prey to the "wrathful divinities" cited by Chogyam Trungpa in his translation of *The Tibetan Book of the Dead.* He described their "ruthless, unyielding quality, not allowing sidetracks of any kind." Surely that had brought me to a habitual state of fear of the Tyrant's authority. His further comment, "If you approach them and try to reshape the situation they throw you back," had also been part of my story.

But now that I knew the Tyrant's attack had been energized by unconscious reactions to these major masculine figures, I could start afresh. Although my parents had vanished from this world, I must free myself from the inner reactions to authority that still preyed on my psyche. The next question was, "if the Tyrant isn't really me, then why believe him when he calls me foolish and weak?" Maybe the Woman in a Coma was afraid to express how she felt, but now I understood that the openness and vulnerability he criticized so harshly was, in fact, a gift. Only if I dared to be vulnerable could I (or anyone else, for that matter) open to true feeling.

As I absorbed these new realizations, the tone of the Tyrant's voice began to change. But he's a wily fellow and though he seemed to have gone on vacation, I still felt his judgmental presence. His angry ranting softened, his words more like those of a controlling parent who pushed me to do what he thought was the "right thing." This subtler presentation made it more difficult to smoke him out. How could I object to his wish for me to act rightly? Surely it was good advice! However, his condescending tone roused my suspicion. This judge obviously thought he knew best what the right thing was. He wasn't suggesting, he was ordering! So I dubbed his new voice The Lord of Discipline.

In my outer life, although I no longer pressured myself so much to "perform," there were still heavy demands on me. I'd been taking Alexander Technique lessons to relieve stress (see Chapter Four of *The Practice of Presence*), and finally determined to leave *Fortune* and train to become an Alexander teacher. Certification was a three-year journey, five days a week, three hours a day, worth every minute and every cent. As my kinesthetic awareness grew (where I am in my body and in space), I began to think differently about this mortal vehicle I lived inside. What, in fact, did it serve and why did I push it around so much? Could this insistence that it do my instant bidding, any time, any place, come from the Lord of Discipline? I decided to speak to him from my body's point of view:

Disciplinarian, why are you always pushing me around?
YOU NEED HELP. YOU NEVER SEE CLEARLY WHAT YOU MUST DO.

And you do?
I SEE WHAT'S NEEDED, WHAT YOU MUST ACCOMPLISH. THEN I TELL YOU WHAT TO DO.

That's fine when you have suggestions, but why do you treat me like a donkey, with beatings and carrots?
THE BODY'S GOT TO DO ITS JOB!

Which is?
FOLLOWING MY ORDERS!

His bossiness challenged me to be more sensitive to my body's needs. Rather than figure out how far I could push myself, I tried to respect the organism and its limitations. That effort elicited a dream: *I got into a taxi and was closing the door when a Sydney Greenstreet character got in the opposite door. I tried to jump out my door fast, but he had a weirdly long arm, which extended out his window, over the top of the car and grabbed me as I got out on the other side.* "What could this possibly mean?" I wondered.

Long arm, why are you coming after me?
TO CATCH YOU.

Why do you want to catch me?
I NEED YOU.

Whatever for?
TO MAKE YOU AN EXAMPLE.

An example of what?
YOU DO THINGS WRONG.

How did you get such a long arm?
IT EXPANDS AND CONTRACTS WHEN NECESSARY.

Like the long arm of the law?
EXACTLY.

So you represent law or judgment or merciless pursuit?
YOU COULD SAY THAT.

What am I guilty of?

I JUST DO WHAT I'M TOLD.

Then why do I feel this is a malevolent pursuit?
THAT'S YOUR PROBLEM.

How can I get away from you?
EXPERIMENT WITH THAT.

You are the servant of the Lord of Discipline?
A HIRED HAND.

Why is this like a movie with Sydney Greenstreet?
I DUNNO.

Am I a guinea pig?
IF I KNEW THAT I WOULDN'T BE HERE.

It disturbed me that the Lord of Discipline felt no sympathy for the body/being that I am, until I realized "feelings" weren't his domain. Like the stern, disparaging Tyrant, he was fruit of certain life experiences. Which meant, thank heaven, that these two scolding fragments weren't me at all! At that thought, a deep wish rose in me to separate from these harsh personas and their negative energy. A feeling/sensation of warmth and gladness flooded me. I determined to be open and put my trust in the present moment.

But, in spite of that resolve, I often felt lost and frightened. Surely if I gave up pushing myself I'd give up living a "principled" life, I thought. What would give me backbone, clarity and purpose if not the discipline of making advance decisions and keeping my word to myself? I asked for help:

Where is the masculine decisiveness that will guide me? Where are you, masculine energy?
RIGHT HERE WHERE YOU ARE.

Can you help me?
WHAT IS HELP?
Don't give me mystery! I need help!

And there was help. It started with my dream life. The familiar tyrants and slaves, torturers and tortured, heroes, cops and criminals mostly disappeared. A new masculine energy entered, first in the guise of a Radiant Boy who pushed a lawnmower with gusto up and down the lawn—a strange image, filled with positive energy. Then another boy, scorned and teased by his friends and classmates, woke me to tears streaming down my face.

Soon dream-encounters with a variety of attractive older men appeared. For example, a dream about a visiting doctor: *Since there was no spare bedroom and my room had twin beds, he slept in the same room with me. No hint of sexual attraction, just doing a friend a favor by putting him up. In the morning, as he walked by my bed on the way to the door, I put out my hand, my eyes still closed in sleep. He took it as he walked toward the door but I wouldn't, couldn't, let go of his hand. My clutch dragged him back, overwhelmed by an unconscious need to stay connected to him.*

Was this the help I needed? Did the sympathetic doctor mean I was I on my way to a cure, a new beginning? A wordless new relationship with my masculine energy unfolded as I wondered what it would be like to be married to someone like him.

Another dream stirred me even more. I wrote about it in *The Practice of Presence*. Because it ushered in another major life change, I'll repeat it here: *A strange young man sat down at a table in a restaurant where a group of us were dining. I noticed something a little remote about him, and when I looked into his eyes, I saw truth there, and heard it in his words. At the same time that there seemed to be a value in our exchange, I felt a strong urge to look away, deny him, pretend he wasn't real, even ignore him. But I stayed face to face with him in the restaurant, respecting him even though I wasn't sure I understood what he was saying. I made an effort to listen in order to keep him sitting there since it was always clear that he might leave at any moment.*

Then the restaurant setting morphed into an outdoor scene in which he and I were climbing a hill on a steep, rocky path. In my dream notes I described it as "coming up from below." Walking behind me, he put his hands on my waist and hips to steady me as I slipped and stumbled, for which I felt grateful. The touch of his hands gave me more strength and energy to go up and I rejoiced in being helped (something I found very difficult to accept in real life). It was clear that he didn't represent a possible new love relationship but, rather, an uncomfortable truth that had to be accepted or he would disappear.

Next morning, I tried to communicate with him:

Who are you?
YOU KNOW ALREADY.

Will you stay a little longer?
DEPENDS ON YOU.

What must I do?
YOU KNOW ALREADY. YOU MUST FACE TRUTH.

But I feel as though I don't quite understand, as though I'll lose contact with you if I stray at all and I'm really not quite clear where I'm supposed to look, or what I'm supposed to accept in order to keep you near.
YOU KNOW ENOUGH TO FOLLOW THE DIRECTION.

Can you help me understand?
TRUST TRUTH. LET IT BE THERE AT THE SAME TIME THAT YOU ARE CONFUSED OR UNACCEPTING OR RESISTANT. IT IS THERE EVEN WHEN YOU DON'T KNOW WHAT IT IS. LEAVE SPACE, LEAVE ROOM FOR IT.

Are you saying that the truth may not be what I think it is?
EXACTLY.

SO WHAT IS TRUTH?
Not an easy question. In fact, as I said in Chapter One, I've been looking for it all my life. But we know something about it. We have a sense of what it is to be honest or deceitful, upright or false. And we can often discover the truth in a specific instance by figuring out what it's not. Truth has a certain vibration which strikes a chord in us any time and any place we hear it. It carries clarity and simplicity. Like the emperor, it wears no clothes.

TRUST AND TRUTH ARE SIMPLE CONCEPTS
The hard part is to accept the guidance of that still, small inner voice that knows more than we do. Why? Unfortunately for us, as my personas insisted, we don't know how to listen. There's too much noise from everywhere, including the static inside us, as our automatic thoughts carry us away from the solid, simple truth of the moment. To protect ourselves and keep things under control, we imagine we are in charge.

TRUTH HAS A TASTE OF ITS OWN

Here's a Hindu story: "A king asked a sage to explain the Truth. In response, the sage asked the king how he would convey the taste of a mango to someone who had never eaten anything sweet. No matter how hard the king tried, he could not adequately describe the flavor of the fruit, and, in frustration, he demanded of the sage, "Tell me then, how would you describe it?" The sage picked up a mango and handed it to the king, saying, "This is very sweet. Try eating it!"

LISTENING IS A PATH

When I hear something arrogant or condescending speak in me, I know I'm off-balance. I don't like it, I'm ashamed of it, I try not to notice it. What a relief to learn it's not me, but a persona! If my head, heart and body are meant to work together as one person, no one part should assume it's better, wiser or more knowing than another.

LEARN TO RECOGNIZE TONES OF VOICE

My head, heart and body speak different languages but I, who seek to be balanced at the center, must listen to them equally. I need to respect the attempts of each to bring me to wholeness. It was only by hearing a subtle arrogance in his tone of voice that I became suspicious of the motives of the Lord of Discipline.

TRUTH IS ALSO ABOUT TRUST

A major question for me, for all of us, is: What can I trust in myself? There is so much uncertainty, self-doubt, fear and a deep need for reassurance, even as we do our best to find our purpose in life and figure out how to relate to others. It's easy to get stuck in black and white judgments about right and wrong. It would be better to offer others and ourselves the benefit of the doubt.

TRUST YOUR BODY

As I said before, we can go a thousand places in our minds, but the body can only do one thing at a time. What a gift! So if we want to return to here and now, one way is to turn our full attention on the body, on where and how it is, on its capacity for taking in the world around us through sensation, on what we're doing and how we are doing it. That's why I love washing dishes. It brings me right back to me-in-the-present. And that warm soapy water feels wonderful!

WHAT RULES DO YOU LIVE BY?

What does your Lord of Discipline demand of you? When do you hear his autocratic voice? In what ways is he 'on your case?' Perhaps you solve problems in several different forms. What are they? Write down the answers to all these and any other questions you have. You can review them later. Make a list of what your "disciplinarian" insists on every time you have an encounter with him.

WHAT IN US LAYS DOWN THE LAW?

Another key to my unmasking of the Disciplinarian was the dialogue about the long arm of the law. To my surprise, the powerful interloper in my taxi was "just a hired hand," and he clearly didn't know much. So who was I really dealing with? Who was behind him? Who called the shots? Who decides what I (or you) should or shouldn't do? And why should we trust him?

Sixteen: The Lord of the Heart

"Lead your own life and not the one projected on you."
Marion Woodman

Marion's advice reached deep into my heart. It invited me to re-examine my fixed attitudes and re-assess much that I'd considered important, and to say goodbye to the Old Masculine personas who had been running my life for so long from underground. The Tyrant, Judge, Persecutor and Slave Driver would have to move off the center of my inner stage.

Not that they'd be gone. It would be naïve to think that viewpoints and attitudes developed and expressed throughout a lifetime could be so easily abandoned. Only conscious awareness and psychic intuition would enable me to identify their maneuvers behind the scenes. Only when I caught sight of them could I say firmly: "That's not me!"

A dream voice had called out to me several times: *IT'S TIME TO FOLLOW A NEW LEADER!* So I pleaded:

New Leader, I want to be with you.
IF YOU WANT ME TO JOIN YOU, YOU'LL HAVE TO MOVE AT A SLOWER PACE AND NOT GET SO MANY THINGS DONE.

But so much is demanded of me!
DON'T BE SO BUSY, SO DIRECTED, SO EXECUTIVE, SO DEDICATED TO GETTING THINGS DONE. WHEN YOU MOVE FROM ONE THING TO ANOTHER SO QUICKLY,

THERE'S NO ROOM FOR ME TO BREATHE IN YOU. I NEED YOU TO HESITATE, TO WONDER, TO WANDER IN THE PARK, TO PAUSE UNDER THE TREES AND HEAR THE BIRDS SING.

I vowed to live with less tension and not push myself so much. But how to extricate myself from a life oriented around achievement? And what would happen to the Hero, who tried so hard to win out against all odds? Even though he had announced his retirement, I suspected he'd continue to engage me in super-efforts, drama and conflict.

As for Mrs. Rigid, surely I'd go on living with her, because she was afraid and needed me to calm her down when life became too uncertain. The Editor was sometimes useful with his ability to cut and paste. The Ferret was helpful at finding things out, but needed a tight leash or he'd start hunting imagined prey. As for the Child, I hoped she would cling to me forever. What's more, I desperately needed her spontaneity and joy. It was my job to see that she wasn't scared out of her mind.

I turned my focus on the friction created between my critical mind and my hardworking, over-pressured body (not to mention feelings and a marginalized instinctive function). How could I renounce my competitive nature, my over-dedication to obligation and the automatic tendency to please or "help" anyone perceived as needy? Surely no matter how hard I tried, I'd be easy victim to the Tyrant's dark authority. What could help me deal with him?

No doubt about it. I needed help. But now that I'd grown suspicious of the Tyrant's voice and that of my other personas, whom could I trust? The inner call to be present to my life might sound at any moment, inviting me to live richly rather than be lived by personas and projections. What could help me hear it better, so I could let go of whatever I was immersed in and re-organize myself more swiftly on a new tack?

Marion had often spoken of the masculine sword of

discrimination. Could it empower me against both the Tyrant and the Pleaser? That way I could honor first what was of greatest value to me and leave the rest for later. I'd need to make conscious choices instead of falling into habitual attitudes and old ways of doing things.

To start with, I experimented with my tendency to be impatient. Although I was often in a hurry to finish what I'd started, I tried to visualize my impatience as a friend—a wake-up call from complete absorption in whatever I was doing. Each time I recognized how I'd been taken over by the driving, bossy energy of the Lord of Discipline, I'd slow down.

I also hated to be interrupted at whatever I was doing. So I began to interrupt whatever habitual situation I was in. Sometimes I'd change the rhythm of my day or force myself to leave work unfinished to walk in the park, or go to sit quietly in another room. Anything to reduce the build-up of my inner pressure-cooker.

Lucky for me, my cat knew better than I when I'd been working too long at the computer! He paid no attention to my narrow focus as he brushed against me a few times. Then, if he received no response, he'd gently nip at my leg to let me know it was time to roll on the floor and play with him.

The hardest task was to interrupt my tendency to push projects all the way to the finish line as fast as possible. Nevertheless, these new experiments induced real changes in my daily life until an ominous new problem surfaced. As some of the pressure I'd put on myself for many years let go, I began to feel tired all the time. Again, I called for help:

New Leader, the effort to stay open in two directions exhausts me! Why am I so tired?
THE DOER, THE HELPER, THE WORKER ...THEY'VE HAD ENOUGH FOR TODAY.

Then how to let go, shift the center, close down?

YOU DON'T WANT TO CLOSE DOWN. YOU NEED TO OPEN EVEN MORE THE DOOR THAT HAS COME AJAR.

But the fatigue continued. I even dreamt about it: *In a college dorm room, I wake up to see a very prim lady with a ramrod straight back across the room from me, sitting on the edge of another bed. Is she a nun or Mrs. Rigid? On the bed between us an unknown woman lies exhausted, unconscious. She's so intertwined with the bedclothes, I didn't even notice her at first.*

In another dream, I pushed an old lady around in a wheelchair wherever I went, paying no attention to her, as if bringing along baggage I couldn't leave behind. Who was I pushing around? Since my habit had been to push myself to get more things done in a day and stretch my energy, was the dream saying some part of me needed to rest? Oh, no! Anything but rest! I feared rest—it might mean I was past my prime. How could I help these exhausted ladies without falling apart?

New leader, can you help me?
WHAT ARE YOU SO AFRAID OF?

Of being less than I can be, of betraying weakness, of discovering this is "the beginning of the end."
ISN'T IT POSSIBLE TO BE SOMETIMES ENERGIZED AND SOMETIMES NOT?

No, because the "not " part is betraying me.
BETRAYING YOU HOW?

Showing me up, sending the wrong message.
WHY DO YOU LIVE BY "ORDEALS? WHY DREDGE UP EVERY BIT OF ENERGY YOU CAN GIVE TO A SITUATION, INSTEAD OF JUST MEETING IT AS IT HAPPENS, MOMENT BY MOMENT?

That's true. All my guns are pointed and ready to fire all the time. Surely that's the Old Masculine, "ready-for-battle" state. Giving it up will be hard.
TAKE HEART. YOU ARE CHANGING. YOU "ALLOW" MORE OFTEN, RATHER THAN INSIST. IN TODAY'S TAI CHI CLASS YOU HELPED WHOEVER SHOWED UP, RATHER THAN SUFFER FROM A SENSE OF FAILURE BECAUSE SEVERAL PEOPLE DIDN'T COME.

That's true. The old mode was: I need to work very hard at teaching so everyone will come back tomorrow. Otherwise I'm a failure!
LISTEN TO YOUR OWN WORDS. WHY ARE YOU A FAILURE?

Because if they don't come again, I didn't convince them.
BUT WHAT HAS CONVICTION TO DO WITH LEARNING TAI CHI? SURELY THEY WANT TO OR THEY DON'T?

If I inspire them enough, they'll work hard at it to receive the light I bring them!
OHO! SO DEEP DOWN YOU WISH TO BRING THE LIGHT. BUT ISN'T THE LIGHT WHAT'S IMPORTANT RATHER THAN HOW YOU BRING IT?

Well, sometimes I feel the light inside me and want to share it.
I AM THE LIGHT THAT SHINES THROUGH YOU, BUT YOU DON'T HAVE TO KINDLE IT OR POWER IT UP. YOUR JOB IS TO STAY OUT OF THE WAY!

With those words I felt a weight had been taken from me. I was no longer expected to accomplish something that, deep down, I knew I wasn't capable of. At the same time, I became curious. Perhaps the murderer in my dreams wasn't always my enemy, or a negative persona like the Tyrant. Could he sometimes represent someone who became angry when I was "inauthentic" or untrue to my nature? I turned again to my guide:

New Leader, can we resolve this? Who is angry when I'm angry?
THERE'S MORE TO THIS THAN MEETS THE EYE.

To whom am I speaking?
WITHIN THE FIRE IS THE ROSE.

So you're saying the fire isn't going to consume me?
YOU COULD PUT IT LIKE THAT.

Why is everything an ordeal?
BECAUSE YOU'RE ALWAYS FIGHTING YOUR WAY INTO EVERYTHING.

Is there a way to escape from ordeal-making?
RETUNE YOURSELF. GIVE UP INSTEAD OF PUSHING THROUGH. FOLLOW ANOTHER LEADER.

At this exchange, my every cell came alive, full of joy and a deep desire to change. I wrote in my journal: *I wish to change into MYSELF! The Wrathful Divinities must live in the head, because my anger seems related to thoughts of how I OUGHT to be, and to Discipline with a capital D. But surely the Peaceful Divinities live in the heart. I wish to kneel before the throne of The Lord of the Heart.*

As this new energy filled me, eyes brimming with tears, I muttered: "I know You are here with me right now." At that moment, an image appeared in my mind of a huge roadside billboard with gigantic red letters that said: **UNDER NEW MANAGEMENT**. Later that day, I took paper and paint to recreate the billboard and post it where I would always see it. An inner shift was taking place. The authoritarian foundation instilled in my psyche by my two fathers and the zeitgeist of the era in which I grew up ebbed away.

Above all, I realized, any obedience to authority must be voluntary, at least for me. I must never again bow to THE ANGRY MASCULINE, the wrathful Tyrant who had so long dominated me, or the Lord of Discipline who had replaced him with a list of rules to live by. My true duty from now on was to follow the promptings of the Lord of the Heart, to open to him and receive his guidance with joy. In order to reaffirm this decision, I wrote a description of what they represented to me:

Rules of the Lord of Discipline:
Punishment for transgression every time.
Watching carefully for mistakes and pointing them out.
Catching the elusive spirit and pinning it down like a butterfly.
Making judgments without forgiveness.
Competition modality with everyone.
Accept no excuses.
Take no prisoners.
Forgive no one.

The Nature of The Lord of the Heart:
Love
Joy
Opening
Sensitivity
Courage to weep
Trust of the Spirit
Natural befriending of others
Sharing what has been given
Valuing what is precious
Letting go into life

I determined to obey the gentler promptings of the Lord of the Heart from now on. But, I wondered, where was the conscious feminine? Not the passive Woman in a Coma who fainted in the face of any ordeal, but an active feminine energy that could help me meet life's challenges.

This was new territory. Since I'd been the family wage earner for some 30 years, grasping for success in what was mostly a man's world, I'd long ago donned pants both literally and figuratively. I seldom wore a dress or thought about my feminine nature. Yet I'd often heard Marion speak of the Conscious Feminine. As she recently explained it: "I don't mean gender. I mean the feminine principle that is living—or suppressed—in both men and women…The feminine is presence, and relatedness, and a heart that can open so that when you meet another person you actually are seeing that person's authentic self." (O magazine interview, September 2009).

Since each of us carries both feminine and masculine energy, and to live well we must find a balance between them, where in myself was there a conscious feminine worthy of accompanying the Lord of the Heart? As I knelt on my prayer stool, meditating the question, an awesome power visited me. Suddenly, as all of me tingled with energy, I recalled the sixth verse of Lao Tsu's *Tao Te King*:

"The Valley Spirit never dies.
It is called the Mysterious Woman.
The gate of the Mysterious Woman
Is the root of heaven and earth.
Draw upon it as you will,
It never runs dry."

The Valley Spirit: feminine energy from the roots of the world! Humble, grateful, my turning thoughts for once completely silenced, I went in to breakfast. As was my custom, I pulled out a

book. It happened to be Marion Woodman's *Ravaged Bridegroom.*
I read: "We come to a crossroads where the little life our ego
controls is shattered by a larger reality." The barriers at the
crossroads, where I'd stood for so many years, had been shattered
indeed!

All that day I felt at home in myself, moving with measured
speed, attending carefully to everything I did. What had earlier
seemed so important no longer dominated my attention. I realized
that the part of me the Tyrant accused of being 'lazy' was simply
overstressed. I promised myself never to push this body/mind
around again. And at that very moment, as my eyes welled with
tears, I knew my vow had been heard by the listener within. I said:

Today I wish to spend with You.
THEN KEEP ME WITH YOU.

Stay with me. Don't leave me. Tell me what to do to keep you here.
**I DON'T DO THAT. I GO WHEREVER YOU GO, AND DO
WHATEVER YOU DO.**

That sudden denial devastated me. Here I was, ready to give
myself over completely to a higher power, to offer myself as I'd
longed to do all my life. But it wasn't enough and it wasn't right. I
asked myself, "Why isn't it acceptable to turn myself over to this
special energy? Something must be up to me in order to keep the
connection alive." I remembered Madame de Salzmann's words:
"You cannot do it, but without you it cannot be done."

A new presence, much larger than I, had invited me to find
a measured pace, rather than live under the daily pressure I forced
on myself. But, "ah, me!" I cried. "What can I do when the Lord of
Discipline moves in and tries to liquidate my new intention?"

That question has lived in me ever since. A new connection
with myself has sometimes seemed to hang by a thread, very
breakable. If I turned away, forgot to breathe into my back, or

drowned in "doing stuff," I was once again at the crumbling edge of an abyss. And only the longing not to lose myself could save me from plunging over it.

How thin, how fragile that thread is. Returning each day to nature helps me remember it. A vitality larger than my own can fill me with new hope, even when the thread seems to have broken; even when I return from very far away.

But, hey, is it ever broken? My attention moves away, attracted elsewhere, even sometimes seized. But isn't it possible that the golden thread is still there? At the merest glimmer of gold in my daily life, I experience an inner shift. When I walk in the park, when a stranger smiles at me, when a child laughs gleefully, when a word or image suddenly touches my heart or a memory reminds me of my wish, I turn, often with anguish, to look again for the thread. And there it is, waiting for me, in the kingdom of the Lord of the Heart.

WHY DO YOU HURRY?
We may not realize how much pressure we put on ourselves, but we can recognize the sense of hurry, the urgency to finish what we're doing and move on to the next thing. It's often a result of our effort to be "good," to do the job well and meet the demands of life with our best effort. That's a good intention but shouldn't demand more of the body than it can give to stay healthy. So ask yourself, what is hurry doing to your nervous system?

NOTICE HOW PRESSURE CUTS OFF RECEPTIVITY
Putting pressure on myself all the time actually interferes with the flow of my life, just like staying out in the cold too long, or eating too much at every meal. If the nervous system has two opposing modes, firing up and quieting down, and I spend 90 percent of my time in the first mode, then I'm clearly off balance.

PUT A LIMIT ON ORDEAL-MAKING DEMANDS

The call to live in a different way resides in all of us. Whether or not we're aware of it, there's a real desire to move away from the automatic pressure with which we meet the demands life brings us. But do we listen to it? In my case, those demands made everything feel like an ordeal. Then I began to notice the reason why: I'd put on pressure to feel I'd "paid" for the right to rest every evening. Is that your habit too? Try to go against pushing yourself around although it may seem like the only way to get things done.

COME ALIVE TO THAT SELF-PUSHING SENSATION

If you can recognize, at any moment, the sense of "efforting," of how you drive yourself against natural feelings and body fatigue, you're halfway to changing the way you operate. Yes, sometimes we have to press on to finish a job, and that's O.K. when we're consciously aware of the need. We can promise ourselves a rewarding time-off later. However, much of the time we just push ourselves habitually, not knowing we're "going against the grain."

CLARIFY WHAT YOU MEAN BY "SUCCESS"

I tended to equate success with marking items off my to-do list. Is that your habitual attitude, too? You might want to reexamine it. As Joan Borysenko so astutely said in Inner Peace for Busy People, "Your to-do list is immortal. It will live on long after you're dead." Decide mindfully what you really want to succeed at. Hopefully it will include taking care of yourself!

REORGANIZE YOUR PRIORITIES

Another way of saying all this is that you need to reorganize your priorities to choose more consciously where you want to invest your life energy. We have a measurable amount of get-up-and-go, not to mention a limited time on earth. If you had only a year left on the planet, how would you want to spend it? Let that be your guide.

INTERRUPTIONS CAN FREE YOU FROM RIGIDITY OF MIND
We all react to being interrupted when we're concentrating on something. But, if you're like me, you might become fixated on whatever you're doing and forget everything else. That includes the soup cooking on the stove as well as tension in your back as you force yourself on to greater efforts. Let go. Be interruptible. And bless the interference that came between you and a too-rigid focus.

MAKE FRIENDS WITH YOUR IRRITATED SELF
Ask yourself what's behind your annoyance. Irritation and impatience can serve as a wake-up call. They are often subtle forms of arrogance. I'm too busy to care but attention is demanded of me, or I deserve to be at the head of the line but I'm stuck in the back, waiting for my turn. Make friends with both of these reactions rather than condemn them. They are members of your cast of characters. Remind yourself that they are I-words that could easily morph from "I am annoyed!" to "I am here."

LEARN TO TOLERATE YOURSELF AS YOU ARE
As Thomas Moore said in *Soul Mates:* "Such love of the soul, sometimes felt as nothing more than tolerance of its unreasonable demands, is the basis for intimacy among people. Honoring that aspect of the soul that is irrational and extreme, we have far fewer expectations of perfection, in ourselves and in others — one of the most corrosive elements in any relationship."

TAKE A DEEP BREATH
The effort to be aware of how I am isn't a one-time thing but a way of living. Whenever you're pressured, notice your breathing. Participate consciously in its rhythm as you become aware of the tension in your body. Release your shoulders, your hands that grip everything too tightly, your clenched belly. Breathe into the tightness and the pain. Notice how your thoughts run on when you don't attend to them. Breathe into your thoughts. Let your small self help release your Whole Self from the prison of habit.

Seventeen: Soul Images

"Enter these enchanted woods, ye who dare!"
George Meredith

I'm a word person—quick to formulate thoughts and ideas, a writer by profession. That's why I was skeptical about what I'd read in psychology books—that image appears first in the mind, before words. But when I began to experiment with making art from the unconscious, I was amazed by the power of image over explanation. While words are an important means of exchange in therapy, the images that appeared in my dreams and waking reverie turned out to be a master key to understanding the power of the unconscious world in my psyche.

At one of my first all-day workshops at the Jung Foundation I met Edith Wallace, who had trained with C.G. and Emma Jung in Zurich. She said each of us has a myth-like story to tell about our childhood and invited us to spend the morning looking for our own story and writing it down. After lunch we were to tear colored tissue paper into small pieces and paste them on a white cardboard.

Like the others, I started, stopped and began again several times, finally producing three different collages that told me nothing to which I could relate. With time to make one more, my hands suddenly seemed to know what to do. First a huge yellow sun appeared at the top, above a forest of blue and black tree trunks. One trunk towered high over the others, rising to the top of the paper and melting into the sun. It was tall and dark but had a bright blue top that bent at an angle over the others as if to protect them.

The black forest reminded me of a scary photograph I'd seen as a child, in a book called *The Poet's Camera*. A dark and terrifying wood with gnarled and twisted trees, shadowy in the early evening light, whose branches seemed to writhe and reach toward the viewer. The caption read: "Enter these enchanted woods, ye who dare!" I didn't know it then, but this first experience of artwork from the unconscious marked the beginning of decades of discovery.

A few months later my daughter invited me to join her in a daylong art-therapy workshop at Pratt Art Institute, where I experimented again. Near the end of the afternoon, exhausted and somewhat resentful that there was one more class to get through, I was asked to make a collage from a huge pile of cutout magazine photos. Already tired of pursuing "ghosts," I began without much enthusiasm, but was soon taken over by that same driven energy as my hands selected forms and colors and glued them swiftly to the paper without planning where they should go.

After an hour of intense activity, I'd made a large rectangular collage divided into four quarters with a central figure. A frightened deer ran rapidly off the upper left-hand corner, above the words RUN! RUN! It reminded me of times I felt overwhelmed, wishing to flee as fast as possible from a difficult situation. I named this terrified instinctive fragment of myself The Frightened Deer.

From then on, my attitude softened towards states of fear. It was time to befriend the deer rather than condemn the fear. In other words, I accepted fear as a fact instead of denying I was afraid or making excuses. Sometimes I'd visualize taking the deer for a walk in the street with my hand reassuringly on its back. I'd walk slowly, never forgetting its presence beside me, or the fact that it was trembling with fear. That's how I re-introduced this country-woods fragment to the city streets and the hurly burly of my life in New York.

On another corner of the same collage was a fiery

explosion. My immediate association was that each demand on me was like a four-alarm fire I had to put out right away. But most shocking was the image at the center of the paper, where a serpent devoured a rose. A closer look showed that that its green coils also formed the leaves below the red flower. The serpent as part of the rose, and the rose being eaten by the serpent. I recalled an image from a poem by William Blake:

> **O Rose thou art sick**
> **The invisible worm.**
> **That flies in the night**
> **In the howling storm:**
> **Has found out thy bed**
> **Of crimson joy:**
> **And his dark secret love**
> **Does thy life destroy.**

Was there some destructive force at work in my longing to be good or in my desire for intense spiritual experiences? Only later did I realize Jung would have answered a resounding "yes," quite simply because everything evokes its opposite. My wish for perfection had called shadow forces into play, represented by an invisible worm at the heart of what I held sacred.

Serpent images began to slither through my dreams. The first snake nightmare saw me fleeing from hundreds of tiny snakes that finally cornered me against the back wall of a large room. Filled with terror, I held up a sieve in front of my face in a desperate attempt to protect myself from them even though I knew they were small enough to wiggle right through its holes.

I was often haunted by the image of Laocoon, the Trojan priest of Apollo who warned his people to beware the Trojan horse. The gods punished him by sending serpents to squeeze him and his children to death. This story was famously represented by a second century BC sculpture I knew well. The vision of the serpent coiled all around the man's body—torso, arms, legs—had burned into my mind. Did my body's aches and pains suggest I was being squeezed by serpent power?

As I listened more intently to dream messages and dialogued with my inner cast of characters, the images began to change. For example, after years of snake nightmares, the snake image was transformed one night from fearsome enemy to sacred presence: *I was sitting on the pebbles of a driveway off a country road. Out of the corner of my eye I saw a HUGE snake, tall and wide as a car, long as a freight train, gliding along the road. As it approached the driveway, I thought it was coming after me and cringed down. But it continued on down the road, enormous and endless, paying no attention to me as it slithered slowly by, a couple of yards from where I sat. Yet I felt it absorbed everything around it, including my existence and my fear.* As the dream ended, I felt a rush of gratitude at the honor of seeing its sacred presence pass by.

But the most amazing snake adventure happened in real life, a few days after my stepfather died. I'd gone on a four-day retreat to Mohonk Mountain House, a beautiful country hotel. For three days I ate gourmet meals, swam in the pristine mountain lake and walked along beautiful mountain paths, in an attempt to recover from the grief and tension of his hospitalization and death.

Here's what happened: On the fourth morning I saw what looked from a distance like a small snake, maybe a foot long, at the side of the path, poised in the air. At least a third of its length stood up off the ground. As I approached it to investigate, I expected it to disappear at any moment. But it never moved. So I figured it was just a dead branch or a child's lost toy, and casually picked up a twig to touch it. Instantly, it slithered into the underbrush. Silent partner to my grief?

Another persistent image that came after my return to New York from Peru was that of a crossroads with heavy wooden beams that barricaded all four directions. I was stranded in the middle.

That recalled my childhood belief that there's *NO WAY OUT*. I wrote in my journal:

> *When I find myself "making nice" to others, I see that at the root I'm doing it because I want to be liked, and attack myself for that. However, when I do something that could be considered "selfish" or put my own interests first while giving the impression I'm thinking of the other, I attack myself for that too! I can't do anything right. There seems to be NO WAY OUT, no acceptance of how I am.*

I was stuck at that same crossroads for years, feeling trapped again and again. Finally, one day when I was stuck there once more, I cried out, "What can I do?" Out of the blue, an inner voice replied: ***TRY UP!*** It was the one direction I'd never thought of. Could I find the way to fly over the roadblocks? My kingdom for a helicopter!

While these experiences were clear illustrations that life wasn't exactly what I thought it to be, my mind couldn't take in the messages. One side of me rejected the possibility that these mysterious images could tell me something I needed to know, while the other part suspected they might hold a world of meaning if only I could give up my rational distaste for their hidden power. That may explain another daytime image: a violent tug of war between two teams. Struggle as hard as they might, neither team ever pulled the other over the edge.

As for creative artwork, although I'd enjoyed a sculpture class one summer as a teenager, it had little place in my adult life. I was unable to draw and didn't want to try. "Do it well or don't do it at all!" had been my motto. But as my inner barriers crumbled. I joined a few friends who painted in a process called Form & Color.

The first rule was to give up knowing what would happen. Next, to refuse to let mental determinations and associations lead the brush, but rather choose whatever color attracted me most, then follow the movement of the brush on paper. The images that appeared were sometimes only meaningful days later. When our little painting group broke up, I couldn't find the courage to paint alone but took the easier path of colored pens and magic markers.

One day I ventured to make the experiment Jung himself had tried: to take a significant image from a dream, hold it in the mind and paint. At the center of a small square of heavy paper I drew a crossroads with four roadblocks. Then I let the colored pens move freely without allowing my thoughts to interfere. The result was a rocket ship or a thick arrow with wings, which rose upward at a diagonal. The whole image flew with tremendous energy toward its own destination, carrying my tiny crossroads along with it. My conviction that there was No Way Out was an illusion.

Why did my problems express themselves in images? As I'd often done before, I turned to James Hillman's complex reasoning for clarification. In *The Thought of the Heart* he writes that "The world is a place of living images, and our hearts are the organs that tell us so." OK. Then why don't I listen to the heart with more respect and less fear of being wrong? Hillman answers with another image: "Crucial to the heart of the lion is that it believes...its thought appears in the world as project, desire, concern, mission. Thinking and doing together...(The lion's) thought does not appear as thought because it emanates like the sun into the world..."

His words called me to a new possibility, obscure but inviting. He goes on to say that the lion's "task of consciousness lies in recognizing...that what it experiences as life, love and the world" is really within itself. Here was my new task, my new direction: to turn away from the search for answers I sought everywhere "out there," in books and people, and look for them in myself.

The lion became my new image. That summer, while attending a Jungian conference in Assisi, I met the gaze of a sorrowful lion outside a 12th century church, high over the valley. Its two front paws were crossed in resignation. The look on its face intimated a thousand years of watching the world suffer. Back home, I painted swathes of bright reds and yellows. As they poured from my brush I began to see a colorful lion at rest.

The heart is for seeing rather than feeling, Hillman often affirms. He questions the validity of the scientist's attitude, which he calls Harvey's heart, or the church's confessional mode, derived from St. Augustine. While confession is also central to therapy, why celebrate it in church or on the client couch, he queries, where "the image is imprisoned in its feeling, rather than the feeling released into its images." An alternative would be that "transference, the mystery of therapy, can...move the heart from its confessional mode of experiencing to a prayerful response to its images—witnessing."

Witnessing. There it was again. I'd heard the suggestion many times from my Gurdjieffian studies and often from Marion Woodman's exercises, but now it took on clearer form. A path from doing to seeing—the path of the Conscious Lion. Could I follow it and live in the world passionately, like the lion? A major thrust of the Gurdjieff teaching is learning "to see what is." And the master himself had said: "Think what you feel, feel what you think."

Gurdjieff and Hillman present a new vision of the growth of Being: essence revealed along the length of a lifetime. I could no longer think of myself as a student of all that was "out there," but a living being in whom the many years of studies and practices have come together. Call it becoming oneself, individuation, following Christ, living the Tao, worshipping the gods or eating the ego. By whatever terminology, Gurdjieff, Jung, the Christian tradition, the Taoists, Hindus and Buddhists I'd studied so assiduously, all pointed me in the same direction: To become who I truly am, a servant of higher energies. And my dialogues and paintings were the living experience of that.

These enigmatic soul images fascinated me even when my understanding of them lagged days, weeks or months behind. For example, a nightmare about a black cat with tall, spindly legs, who protected me from a nasty two-headed hydra of a poisonous worm, left me wondering, what was I doing wrong? But a friend suggested the two heads of the worm might represent two energies that were beginning to relate to each other in me. Once more, my assumptions were turned upside down.

On another occasion, my thoughtless doodles with colored pens produced a centipede. When I looked it up, I discovered the image of the centipede is taboo for the Hopi and a symbol of power to the Anasazi, who say it travels between the spirit world and the physical world. An internet source offered this: "The centipede likely symbolizes a single pole ladder, and indicates that the human is making a journey to the spirit world." I could no longer doubt that these images were connecting me with a world beyond my conscious mind.

Another transformative discovery came that fall in an exercise at the end of a daylong workshop with Marion Woodman. She asked us to pair up, one of us to curl up in a ball on the floor with closed eyes and look for an image in the body; the other, in my case a friendly stranger, was there to witness my efforts and protect me from crashing into other pairs if we moved around.

Down onto the cold marble floor I went, looking for an image. The Great Jade stone floated into my mind. The jewel within which, if one dared look long enough, one saw one's own true nature. A moment later I stood up in amazement as a warm sensation swept through my whole body and the realization filled me: *I AM THE STONE! It's not in some valley beyond the Himalayas or deep in a cave, guarded by a dragon, but right here in me!* Shaken and filled with joy, I felt every cell vibrate to this extraordinary new revelation.

In a recent encounter with Marion, the morning after she received a Lifetime Achievement Award from the University of Toronto, she invited us to join in a similar exercise. Again we partnered up, one person to stretch out on a blanket on the floor and find a significant image and place it somewhere in the body; the other to witness and protect.

My mind was a complete blank as I lay down. The well of images had dried up. Wait! Suddenly, in my mind's eye, a little girl came running toward me, arms wide open to embrace and be embraced by me. Was it the 8-year-old girl I left behind when I moved from the country I loved to the city I hated? Tears filled my closed eyes and flowed down my cheeks. When Marion suggested we begin to move with the image and allow it to move in us, I stood up and wrapped my arms around the hugging child and danced with her in exaltation.

Later, when Marion asked for questions, I spoke up: "I know in my mind how much I need to be open to feeling," I said. "So why can't I open more often?" She looked at me with far-seeing eyes that saw beyond the ego's barriers. "It's important to respect your difficulty," she answered. "There may be a very good reason for it." Then, after a pause: "Trust the psyche."

The next morning I wrote in my journal: *Have I walked through a door into another life? I could hardly sleep last night but finally dozed off and woke to this Being-Sensation, my whole body vibrating with life. What else can I call it? One Mind/Body to be honored and attended. How tragic it would be not to pay attention, not to give it room in my daily life. Words fail—because this is not a "part" of me, but the real living Presence of me. And my daily maneuverings either obscure or affirm this reality. For who am I but a busy shadow circling around this substance?*

It's not that I haven't had experiences of "Being" before, of "I" descending into " me." But this is so much more <u>carnal</u>! I must give up the way I looked at things before, all my attitudes and assumptions, as if I understood the Great Work of a lifetime! How can I stay in this freshly discovered world, to live a new life of honor and attention to this Being that I am? Not to wander so far, become so lost in the momentary meanderings of my day, my mind, my psyche. Not to turn my life over to the Organizer, Judge and Critic or even the Mindless Little Girl.

"Trust the psyche," Marion had said. And that's what I've tried to do ever since.

FIND YOUR PATH
Many creative experiences can connect us with our unconscious inner world: painting, collage, sculpture, dance, theater, or any free art expression, as well as written dialogues. To find what works best for you, think back to what you loved to do many years ago. Perhaps one summer you took pottery classes like me. Or you loved to draw, and carried a notebook with you everywhere you went. Or you danced on the grass one night, by the light of the moon.

TAKE AN IMAGE INTO MOVEMENT
It doesn't matter whether you sit quietly until one of your images appears, then dance it, paint it, write about it, squeeze it through your fingers with clay or build stones into houses as Jung did. What's important is to find the means to take your image into movement as your conscious mind follows where another leads you.

DON'T BELIEVE YOUR OLD STORIES
Some people insist they have no artistic talents. I always hated to draw because no matter how carefully I tried, my drawings came out childish and inaccurate. However, once I let go into painting without rules, without expecting to make anything look "real" or "beautiful," a world of possibilities appeared. I was free to mix and dab brilliant colors, creating marvelous swirls that reflected something young and joyous I hadn't felt for years.

SING FROM THE HEART
You may think you can't, but I know it isn't true. Everyone has a voice, small or large, hesitant or powerful. It's just that we don't always dare to listen to it. Especially if we've been laughed at and told we couldn't carry a tune. (Why do we always believe what other people tell us?) Sound out sometime when you're alone. Sing in the shower, or join in with your favorite recorded song. Sooner or later, begin to hum your own song and listen to your own voice.

BE PLAYFUL
We need to discover playfulness all over again and learn to allow the unknown to happen. It's time to give up the "I don't do that anymore because I'm grown up" attitude. Watch children at play. (Not organized sport, which is full of rules and ego competition.) They don't think of it as the opposite of work. Work is play for them and they work at play.

CREATIVITY LIVES IN EVERY CHILD'S NATURE
Notice how they make up their own games; how one idea flows from another. My four-year-old grandson builds huge Lego structures, then crows with joy as he kicks them to pieces. What's more, it's logical. Everything has to crumble so he can build something new! The Indian gods of creation and destruction knew that just as he does. But we elders have forgotten. We hold on and hold back.

THE GODS OFFER US TREASURES EACH DAY
Robert Johnson, in Living Your Unlived Life, reminded us of the Indian monkey-god Hanuman, who offered a fruit each day to Rama the king. Rama, too busy with affairs of state, carelessly tossed them behind his throne. Only when his servants discovered a pile of jewels among the rotting fruit did Rama realize that each had contained a jewel. Adds Johnson, "At the back of each person's throne there lies an accumulating heap of gems...unlived potentials." Seek yours out.

CARRY A REMINDER WITH YOU
Most of the time we forget we are many-sided. But both our personas and our deep longing can teach us that, truly, we are not 'one.' So look for what someone in you treasures, even if a critical persona thinks it's childish. For example, one part of you might treasure a rounded stone, a swirling shell, a faded flower. Keep it in your pocket to remind yourself that "there's more to this than meets the eye," as my inner voices told me. (P. 181)

MAKE IT THEATRICAL
Sacred drama is one of the oldest forms that connect with unknown forces in and around us. Centuries ago, actors presented every aspect of human triumph and tragedy to their audience. That way, everyone's sins and virtues were exposed without anyone having to admit to them in public. Even today theater tells us who we are. While we often accuse people of "acting out," it's useful to act out in private with the conscious aim of understanding what's going on in your inner life. Carefully, of course, so the gods of theater don't run away with you!

JUNG SHOWED US THE WAY
"I took great care to try to understand every single image, every item of my psychic inventory, and to classify them scientifically...and above all, to realize them in actual life. That is what we usually neglect to do. We allow the images to rise up and maybe we wonder about them but ...we do not take the trouble to understand them." (MDR)

Epilogue :
The Wounder and the Wounded are One

"You yourself are a conflict that rages in itself and against itself in order to melt its incompatible substances, the male and the female, in the fire of suffering, and thus create that fixed and unalterable form which is the goal of life...We are crucified between the opposites and delivered up to the torture until the "reconciling third' takes shape. Do not doubt the rightness of the two sides within you, and let whatever may happen, happen. The apparently unendurable conflict is proof of the rightness of your life."

C. J. Jung (Letter to Frau Frobe)

This morning I felt close to the end of my life. The end of a chapter is taking place. Maybe it will lead to a new beginning, maybe not. But in any case, on some level, I need to wrap up the old life, put my house in order and open to my inner house, my true home. How can I let more of myself into my day at all times and at any time?

The wish to be true to myself, to be who I am, has always been the underlying motif of my search. Now life has taught me, willy-nilly, both what I lack and where my treasure lies. But it would be a mistake to think the exploration is over. As any psychologist knows, the psyche is deeper and wider than anyone can imagine. We have more hells and heavens, more devils and angels in us than we have any idea.

And does the dialogue between the wounder and the wounded parts ever end? I suspect not. Recently the voice of the Tyrant reappeared to scold me. So I said:

Why did you say so scornfully, "You klutz!" I saw a paperclip on the kitchen table and put it away. Minutes later I needed a paperclip, but couldn't find where I'd put it. Do you accuse me because I forgot where I put it or are you saying I should have known ahead of time I'd need it?
IT DOESN'T MATTER.

Why doesn't it matter?
BECAUSE YOU ALWAYS MAKE MISTAKES.

I thought we talked some of this out years ago and came to a new relationship.
YOU CANNOT RELATE TO ME.

Why not?
BECAUSE I'M A FIGMENT.

What does that mean?
I'M A CAST-OFF PIECE THAT DOESN'T GO AWAY.

But why do you call me names?
BECAUSE THAT'S WHAT I KNOW HOW TO DO.

So every time I make a mistake you will call me names?
SOMETHING LIKE THAT.

What if I don't want you to hurt me or attack me any more? Is there anything I can do about that?
TALK TO ME MORE OFTEN.

You mean in the midst of action, while you are making your nasty comments?
EXACTLY.

So the exploration isn't over just because I've lived through years of discovery or published a book on presence. Not at all. Just this morning, overcome with emotion, I turned my attention to what was taking place in me. And a weeping voice asked from very far away:

Why am I not received? I've loved so much, I've cared for so many. Where is the recognition, the return?
I hear you, sufferer. I recognize your pain in my blood and bones. But how about joy?

That's true. Loving and caring have been full of joy as well as pain. But who is there to care for me?
Dearest, I suspect that's <u>my</u> job.

The opposing forces I experienced within myself were persona fragments so polarized against each other it seemed impossible they could ever come together: Wounder and Wounded, Tyrant and Slave, Terrorist and Tortured Hero, Scorner and Scorned, Masculine and Feminine, Father, Mother and Child. Nevertheless, they spoke the language of all the feeling-states I've lived through: Affection and Arrogance; Joy and Grief; Fear and Satisfaction; Anger and Depression; Jealousy and Selflessness; Eros and Agape.

Wise teachers from many traditions have said that someday the Two could become One. Does that mean the knife twisted in my wound is, in fact, the sword of discrimination, my own masculine authority turned against me? I suspect that's what happened. The harsh criticism I met or interpreted from parents and teachers in childhood and youth fed a hypercritical self-image that made my life miserable as I judged others and myself by impossible standards. This also created a victim or sufferer who was unacceptable when she didn't meet the imposed standards. In other words, like many other people, I harbored a perfectionist super-ego and an inadequate servant.

That meant I had to be better or different, either by pleasing others so they wouldn't notice my faults or by radically improving myself to win an A for Acceptable. Enter the Tyrant in the guise of the black-robed judge, the whip-cracking slave-driver and the Nazi torturer wielding his knife. Who would defend the Frightened Child? With a swish of his cape, Superman, the achiever appeared, along with the courageous Hero. Mrs. Rigid would program every minute towards success, and the Ferret would figure it all out, while the Woman in a Coma lay back and refused to act.

As my dialogues and studies brought me into closer contact with these rather extreme personas and I experienced their messages consciously, the Tyrannical Judge lost some of his power. He sent replacements: Mrs. Critical Attitude and the Editor were part of a team dedicated both to improve me and to set the world straight.

Gradually a new view of the endless War Within replaced the old. I began to realize that, at any given moment, I affirmed only one side of myself and denied the other. Either I functioned in an active, competent, busy, problem-solving mode or withdrew from it, becoming quiet and receptive. Either the active mind or the meditative mind was in charge. So for a long, long time I tried to figure out which of these two was the Real Me, convinced that one must be "right" and the other "wrong."

This tug-of-war lasted for decades, accompanied by physical pain and mental distress. Even so, my efforts to understand it received a lot of help: The Gurdjieff teaching, the centering power of the daily practice of Tai Chi, Jungian psychology with its Active Imagination experiments, prayer, meditation, and the neuro-physical awareness generated by the Alexander Technique, all contributed to a growing sense of inner freedom.

Long ago, in a message that has always sent shivers down my spine, Gurdjieff warned that a whole lifetime could go by in "an endless hesitation in the same place" (*In Search of the Miraculous*). He also said that: "Only he will deserve the name of man and can count upon anything prepared for him from Above, who has already acquired corresponding data for being able to preserve intact both the wolf and the sheep confided to his care" (*Meetings with Remarkable Men*). Marion Woodman's statement that the wounders and the wounded are one began to make sense at last. Wolf and sheep; wounder and wounded; Tyrant and Child; the murdering masculine and the Woman in a Coma: Two energies need to come together in me, in all of us. And both Gurdjieff and Jung insist that a third energy is needed to transform our lives.

Crucified between affirmation and denial, between active and passive modes of being, I might have spent a lifetime seesawing from one to the other without connecting the two, a victim of both. But at last, as a result of my dialogues, these two aspects of myself softened towards each other. The Tyrannical Judge pointed out more gently what needed to be done, helped make decisions, gave hints and even, at times, useful orders. The child brought joy and freshness, lightness of body, gentleness of feeling, good health. And the Lord of the Heart brought me home.

You could even say I was re-educated by my personas! Many scolded me, judged me and despised me, while others cheered me on. On one level, I recognize that the Tyrant, the black-robed Judge, the Critic, the Slave-driver, Mrs. Rigid, the Ferret, the Editor, the Pleaser, the Hero, the Savage, the Nazi, Superman, the Blonde Eyeful and the Frightened Child were fixed personality fragments. But they also carried my own energy, sometimes draining it away, sometimes bringing me life.

Most of them disapproved of me, and whatever I did. They spent their time (and my life energy) keeping me in line. For a long time it seemed that all these shadow figures were after me, and nobody was "on my side." But that wasn't quite true because, although Superman and the Hero exhausted me with their compulsive attempts to solve all problems, they really tried to help.

And the Child was starved for love and comfort that only I could give myself.

As I became more conscious of the conflict, the Tyrant stopped wanting to punish all the time and the child stopped insisting that each moment be an outstanding experience. While the Tyrant would always be critical and envision an enormous to-do list, longer than the length of a day, sometimes the child was allowed to say, "To hell with all this, I'll do something else." And sometimes I could quietly turn away from both and take time to do nothing.

In the space between them a real person emerged, a growing human being in search of the meaning of life, who learned to recognize these personas, and many other occupants of my psyche besides. There are surely more depths to plumb and, perhaps, more heights to reach, as well as unrecognized parts of myself that haven't yet been loved, accepted or integrated.

Today I asked myself, "How do I want to live?" The reply from deep inside was instantaneous: *"In love!"* What does that mean? To be where I love, to love what I do, not to force or drive myself. No longer young, I recognize the hesitations, memory lapses and temporary imbalances of the body as signposts on the road. How much time do I have left in this vibrant life I'm now living? Why is it so difficult to accept that I am what I am until life comes to a stop? That what's important is being here, living it. Not accomplishing something, not "doing."

As I left the Toronto conference, Marion walked in. We sat together for a moment on a bench near the door and I began to tell her what I must now give up in order to go forward. She fixed me with those eagle eyes and asked, "Why give anything up?" Her question still resounds in me. Why give things up? Be wary of fixed attitudes and determined decisions that reduce your possibilities. Be yourself. Find yourself in what you do. Take yourself into what you do.

I've looked into the Great Jade stone of the Masters, my body-self, and there is no stone, only this Being that I am. The little girl runs toward me with her arms open and I, rejoicing, open mine to receive her embrace. At another moment she fades and moves backwards, like the rewinding of a film. "No! No! No!" I cry. "I don't want to lose you. Stay with me. Why do you go? Is the old life closing around me?" And the Lord of the Heart answers: *WAIT AND LISTEN. BEAR THE BURDEN. BE PRESENT TO IT AND TO YOUR LIFE.*

So I rejoice whenever the Lord of the Heart chooses to abide briefly in the living temple that I am, an experience of great spiritual delicacy. Or when the Valley Spirit settles deep into my belly during Tai Chi or walks in the park. When I remember to sink the *chi* and "stand like a tree," she pulls me down from the whirling thoughts in my head, filling me with energy, rooting me in the earth.

Will they ever come together? Will there be an inner marriage between the Lord of the Heart and the Valley Spirit? That was the secret aim of alchemists who sought to transform base metals into gold and the avowed goal of the Jungian individuation process. But I've no idea. Although I've had a few marriage dreams in recent years (including one in which the bridegroom never showed up), I'll take life as it comes.

Today, on my seventy-fifth birthday, I recognize what has become fact for me: there's nowhere to go in the future because the present is complete unto itself. As the saying goes, the journey, not the arrival, is what matters. Remembering again the card game we played in Peru, endlessly amassing and losing cards, I ask myself and my readers: "With all our busyness, who are we working for?"

Lucky me. Now, at least sometimes, I know who I'm working for. But I can only offer myself to the extent my understanding permits at any given moment. I hear myself say my habitual Pleaser question of many years, "How'm I doing?" So I try to say, instead, "Here I am." And when I affirm that, I honor my truth, my authentic Being, and all those bits and pieces gathered over 75 years spent in the tumult of living.

"And then the knowledge comes to me that I have space within me for a second, timeless, larger life."

R. M. Rilke ("I love my Being's dark hours")

ACKNOWLEDGEMENTS

Jeanne de Salzmann long ago told me, when I was trying to express my gratitude to her, "There is only one way to thank." Considering this, I hope I've been able to be useful to others as I traced a path for myself. I wish to express a deep gratitude to her and to the many teachers, living and dead, ancient and modern, known and unknown, whose words and example have helped me explore the meaning and aim of my existence. Outstanding among them, my mother has been an inspiration for many years. G. I. Gurdjieff's teaching has thrown new light on everything I've studied. In more recent years, the writings of C. G. Jung and the work of Jungian analysts Marion Woodman, Joseph Wagenseller and James Hollis, among others, have offered practical help and accompanied me on my way. My three children have educated me in who I am. Thanks also go to writer Luis Fernando Llosa who helped sharpen my prose; to my Tai Chi partner, Herb Cohen, who led me by the hand through the process of publishing this book; to Jim Sarfati who designed the cover; and to my webmaster, John Hemminger, who also took the photo on the back cover.

ABOUT THE AUTHOR

Patty de Llosa has led group classes, daylong workshops and weeklong intensives in the Gurdjieff work, T'ai Chi and Taoist meditation and teaches the Alexander Technique both privately and in group classes. Among recent public venues are Northern Pines Health Resort, the Peruvian Aikido Association, the Lake Conference Center, Columbia University Graduate Theater Program and the Society for Experimental Studies, Toronto.

After graduating from Swarthmore College, Ms. de Llosa worked as a reporter for *Time Magazine* for six years. She married a Peruvian and raised three children in Lima. When her husband became governor of Loreto province, she served as president of The Green Cross, bringing treatment and medicines to the needy in the Amazon jungle, and coordinating with the Peace Corps a summer visit of American doctors and young people to help build roads and schools there. Returning to Lima she founded and ran a school for eight years—the first foreign chapter of the United Nations pre-school, International Playgroup.

De Llosa returned to New York in 1979, where she worked for six years as managing editor of *American Fabrics & Fashions*, then as associate editor of *Leisure Magazine*, a Time Inc. startup, moving on to *Fortune Magazine* for thirteen years, where she became deputy chief of reporters. She retired in 1999 to take the three-year teacher-training program at the American Center for the Alexander Technique, while working halftime as communications director of internet startup e-academy, inc. and writing her first book, ***The Practice of Presence: Five Paths for Daily Life*** (Morning Light Press, 2006). You can talk to her at practiceofpresence.com and tamingyourinnertyrant.com.

BIBLIOGRAPHY

Borysenko, Joan Z., *Inner Peace for Busy People: 52 Simple Strategies for Transforming Your Life*, Hay House, Carlesbad, CA, 2001

Campbell, Joseph, *The Hero With a Thousand Faces*, Princeton University Press, Princeton, NJ, 1990.

De Llosa, Patty, *The Practice of Presence: Five Paths for Daily Life*, Morning Light Press, Sandpoint, ID, 2006

De Salzmann, Jeanne, *The Reality of Being*, Shambhala, Boston, 2010

Edinger, Edward, *Ego and Archetype*: *Individuation and the Religious Function of the Psyche*, Shambhala, Boston, 1992

T. S. Eliot, *The Four Quartets,* Harcourt, Orlando, FL, 1943

Frye, Northrop, *Late Notebooks, Vol. V, 1982-1990*, Edited by Robert Denham, University of Toronto Press, 2000

The Gospel According to Thomas, A. Guillaumont, Henri Charles Puech, Gilles Quispel, and Walter Till (translators), Evangelium nach Thomas, Leiden, 1959.

Gould, Joan, *Spinning Straw into Gold: What Fairytales Reveal about the Transformations in a Woman's Life*, Random House, New York, 2005

Gurdjieff, G. I., *All & Everything*: *Beelzebub's Tales to His Grandson*, Viking Arkana, New York, 1992. (Audiotape, MP3 format, at www.TraditionalStudiesPress.com.) ---. *Meetings with Remarkable Men*, E.P. Dutton, New York, 1974.

Hillman, James, *Healing Fiction*, Spring Publications, Woodstock CT, 1995
---, *The Soul's Code: In Search of Character and Calling*, Warner Books, New York, 1997.
---, *The Thought of the Heart and the Soul of the World*, Spring Publications, Woodstock CT, 1997
---, Jungian Psychoanalytic Association, Philip Zabriskie Lecture: "Aphrodite's Justice." November, 2008

Hollis, James, *Swamplands of the Soul: New Life in Dismal Places*, Inner City Books, Toronto, 1996
---, *Finding Meaning in the Second Half of Life*, Gotham Books, New York, 2005
---, *Why Good People Do Bad Things: Understanding Our Darker Selves*, Gotham, New York, 2007
---, *What Matters Most: Living a More Considered Life*, Gotham, New York, 2009.

Johnson, Robert, *Owning Your Own Shadow: Understanding the Dark Side of the Psyche*, HarperCollins, New York, 1993
---, with Jerry M. Ruhl,, *Balancing Heaven and Earth: A Memoir of Visions, Dreams, and Realizations*, HarperCollins, New York, 1998
---, *Living Your Unlived Life: Coping with Unrealized Dreams and Fulfilling Your Purpose in the Second Half of Life*, Tarcher/Penguin, New York, 2007

Jung, C. G., *The Collected Works of C.G. Jung (CW)* in 20 Volumes: H. Read, M. Fordham, G. Adler, W. McGuire, editors,

Bollingen Series XX, Princeton University Press, NJ, 1992
---, *Memories, Dreams, Reflections*, Vintage, New York, 1963
---, *Man and His Symbols*, Doubleday, New York 1964
---, *C. G. Jung Speaking: Interviews and Encounters*, Ed. William McGuire and R.F.C. Hull, Bollingen Series, Princeton University Press, Princeton NJ 1997

Kalsched, Donald, *The Inner World of Trauma: Archetypal Defenses of the Personal Spirit,* Routledge, London, 1996
---, interview by Daniela Sieff, *Caduceus Journal*, 2006

Mallasz, Gina, *Talking with Angels,* Daimon, Zurich, 1988

Merton, Thomas, *No Man is an Island*, Harvest, New York, 2002.

Moore, Thomas, *Soul Mates: Honoring the Mystery of Love and Relationship,* HarperCollins, New York, 1994

Mundy, Talbot, *Om: The Secret of Ahbor Valley,* Kessinger Publishing, Whitefish, MT, 2004.

Ouspensky, P. D., *In Search of the Miraculous*, Harcourt, New York, 2001.

Reymond, Lizelle, with Sri Anirvan: *To Live Within: A woman's spiritual pilgrimage in a Himalayan hermitage,* Rudra, Portland, OR, 1995.

The Essential Rumi, Coleman Barks (translator), with John Moyne, A. J. Arberry and Reynold Nicholson, Castle Books, Edison, NJ, 1997.

Smith, Manuel J., *When I Say No, I Feel Guilty,"* Bantam, New York, 1975

The Tibetan Book of the Dead, Chogyam Trungpa and Francesca Fremantle (translators), Shambhala, Boston, 1992

--- or *The Great Book of Liberation Through Understanding in the Between*, Robert Thurman (translator), Bantam, New York, 1994

Von Franz, Marie-Louise, *The Way of the Dream,* DVD, The Marion Woodman Foundation, 2008.

Whitmont, Edward C., with Sylvia Brinton Perera, *Dreams, A Portal to the Source*, Routledge, London, 1989

Woodman, Marion, *Addiction to Perfection: The Still Unravished Bride*, Inner City Books, Toronto, 1982.
---, *The Ravaged Bridegroom: Masculinity in Women,* Inner City Books, Toronto, 1990.
---. with Robert Bly, *The Maiden King: The Reunion of Masculine and Feminine*, Owl Publishing, New York, 1999.
---, *Bone: Dying into Life*, Viking Penguin, New York, 2000.

Welch, William J., *What Happened In Between: A Doctor's Story,* Braziller, New York, 1972.

Zweig, Connie and Jeremiah Abrams, editors, *Meeting the Shadow: The Hidden Power of the Dark Side of Human Nature*, Jeremy P. Tarcher, Los Angeles, 1991.

CPSIA information can be obtained at www.ICGtesting.com
Printed in the USA
BVOW041422011111

275005BV00001B/98/P